The Complete
FLY FISHERMAN™

Fly Rod
Gamefish

THE FRESHWATER SPECIES

By Dick Sternberg

Credits

CY DECOSSE INCORPORATED

President/COO: Nino Tarantino
Executive V. P./Editor-in-Chief: William B. Jones
Chairman Emeritus: Cy DeCosse

FLY ROD GAMEFISH: The Freshwater Species
By: Dick Sternberg

Executive Editor, Outdoor Group: Don Oster
Fishing Products Director: Dick Sternberg
Technical and Photo Advisor: David Tieszen
Editorial Consultants: John Randolph, Ben Streitz,
  David Tieszen
Project Manager: Tracy Stanley
Copy Editor: Janice Cauley
Associate Creative Director: Bradley Springer
Senior Desktop Publishing Specialist: Joe Fahey
V. P. Photography & Production: Jim Bindas
Studio Manager: Marcia Chambers
Principal Photographer: William Lindner
Staff Photographer: Mike Hehner
Photo Assistants: Tom Heck, Mike Hehner, Jim Moynagh,
  David Tieszen
Photo Editor: Anne Price
Senior Production Manager: Gretchen Gundersen
Production Staff: Laura Hokkanen, Tom Hoops,
  Jeanette Moss, Mike Schauer
Illustrators: Maynard Reece, Jon Q. Wright

President/COO: Philip L. Penny

Contributing Individuals and Agencies: Tom Andersen;
  Dan Bailey's Fly Shop – John Bailey; Berkley; C. C. Filson
  Co. – Jim Rex; D. B. Dunn; G. Loomis – Bruce Holt;
  Helly Hansen – Dave Fuller; Hobie Outback – Bill
  Horner; Hobie Sunglasses – Dennis Bush; O. Mustad &
  Son; The Orvis Co. – Paul Ferson, Tim Joseph, Tom
  Rosenbauer; Ross Reels; Sage Manufacturing Corporation
  – Marc Bale, Don Green, David T. Low, Jr.; St. Croix Rod
  Company – Rich Belanger, Jeff Schluter; Scott Fly Rod
  Company – Todd Field, Stephen D. Phinny; Simms;
  3M/Scientific Anglers – Jim Kenyon

Printed on American paper by: R. R. Donnelley & Sons Co.
99 98 97 96 / 5 4 3 2 1

DICK STERNBERG is widely recognized as one of the country's top fisherman/ biologists. His unique ability to explain game-fish behavior in an easily understandable manner has helped millions of anglers catch more fish.

Also available from the publisher:

Fly-Fishing Equipment & Skills, Fly Fishing for Trout in Streams, Fly-Tying Techniques & Patterns

Library of Congress
Cataloging-in-Publication Data

Sternberg, Dick.
Fly rod gamefish: the freshwater species /
by Dick Sternberg.
  p. cm. – (The Complete fly fisherman)
Includes index.
ISBN 0-86573-060-1
1. Freshwater fishes. 2. Freshwater fishes--Identification.
3. Fly fishing.   I. Title. II. Series.
QL624.S76 1996
597. 092'973--dc20   96-8753

CONTENTS

INTRODUCTION ···· 4

TROUT & SALMON ···· 7

TROUT & SALMON BASICS ···· 8
POPULAR SALMONID
SPECIES ···· 12
SENSES ···· 18
FEEDING & GROWTH ···· 21
SPAWNING ···· 22
HABITAT ···· 26
WEATHER ···· 28

LARGEMOUTH BASS ···· 31

LARGEMOUTH BASS BASICS ··· 32
SENSES ···· 35
FEEDING & GROWTH ···· 36
SPAWNING ···· 38
HABITAT ···· 41
WEATHER ···· 44

SMALLMOUTH BASS ···· 49

SMALLMOUTH BASS BASICS ··· 50
SENSES ···· 52
HABITAT ···· 54
FEEDING & GROWTH ···· 58
SPAWNING ···· 60
WEATHER ···· 62

PIKE & MUSKIE ···· 67

PIKE & MUSKIE BASICS ···· 68
SENSES ···· 74
SPAWNING ···· 78
FEEDING & GROWTH ···· 80
HABITAT ···· 86
WEATHER ···· 88

SUNFISH ···· 90

SUNFISH BASICS ··· 93
BLUEGILL ···· 94
REDEAR SUNFISH ···· 96
LONGEAR SUNFISH ···· 98
REDBREAST SUNFISH ···· 100
PUMPKINSEED ···· 102

OTHER FLY ROD SPECIES ···· 104

CRAPPIES ···· 106
ROCK BASS ···· 110
WHITE BASS ···· 112
STRIPED BASS ···· 116
WALLEYE ···· 118
LAKE WHITEFISH ···· 120
AMERICAN SHAD ···· 122

INDEX ···· 124

Introduction

Artificial flies are tied to imitate items in the diet of most every gamefish; consequently most every gamefish can be caught on a fly.

Although trout are by far the most popular fly rod gamefish, warmwater species like bass, crappies and sunfish are closing the gap. Not only will these fish readily take flies, there are times when they prefer flies to other types of lures. Some coolwater fish, such as pike, muskies and even walleyes, are also starting to develop a following among flyfishermen.

Fly Rod Gamefish will acquaint you with the 37 freshwater fish species most commonly taken by fly fishing. Besides showing you how to identify them, we'll discuss aspects of their biology that will help you put them on the end of your line.

The first thing you need to know about any gamefish is the type of habitat it prefers. What kind of cover is it normally found in? What is its preferred water temperature range? How much dissolved oxygen does it require? What are its preferences in regard to water clarity, depth and current? A good understanding of these habitat requirements is an invaluable fishing tool.

Another indispensible tool is knowledge of a fish's spawning habits. Many fish are most vulnerable to fly fishing around spawning time. Not only do they feed heavily just before spawning, they're usually in shallow water, where flies are most effective. Besides knowing when they spawn, you must be able to recognize a typical spawning area.

Understanding a fish's diet is a big help in getting them to bite, because you can buy or tie flies that imitate the predominant food items. In most cases, you don't have to match them exactly, but it helps to present a fly that approximates the natural food in size, shape and color.

Knowing how fish use their senses to detect danger and find prey can help refine your presentation. For example, the noise and splash from a diver or popper may spook a wary rainbow trout, but attract an aggressive pike or bass.

Information on fish age and growth, in itself, may not help you catch them, but it is of great interest to many anglers, as is the listing of the current fly rod world records (all tippet classes included). Putting the biological information in this book to work for you could make you the next record holder.

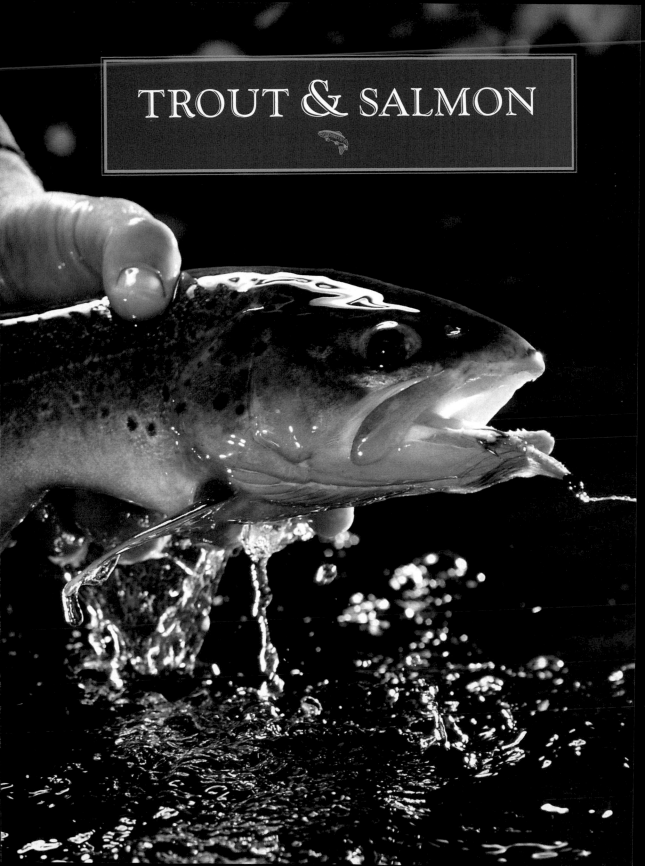

TROUT & SALMON

Trout & Salmon Basics

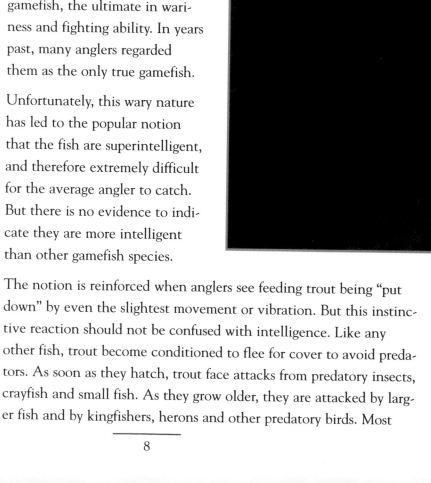

Trout and salmon have long been considered superior gamefish, the ultimate in wariness and fighting ability. In years past, many anglers regarded them as the only true gamefish.

Unfortunately, this wary nature has led to the popular notion that the fish are superintelligent, and therefore extremely difficult for the average angler to catch. But there is no evidence to indicate they are more intelligent than other gamefish species.

The notion is reinforced when anglers see feeding trout being "put down" by even the slightest movement or vibration. But this instinctive reaction should not be confused with intelligence. Like any other fish, trout become conditioned to flee for cover to avoid predators. As soon as they hatch, trout face attacks from predatory insects, crayfish and small fish. As they grow older, they are attacked by larger fish and by kingfishers, herons and other predatory birds. Most

stream fishermen have seen dead trout along the bank with gaping beak wounds in their heads. The wariness of trout also results from natural selection; those that lack wariness do not live to reproduce.

The main thing that distinguishes trout and salmon from other gamefish is their preference for cold water. Although temperature preferences vary among trout and salmon species, most need water temperatures from 50° to 65°F, and avoid temperatures above 70°. This requirement means they live only in streams or lakes fed by springs or snow melt, or in lakes with plenty of cold, well-oxygenated water in the depths.

Trout and salmon belong to the family *Salmonidae* and are referred to as *salmonids*. Besides trout and salmon, the family includes grayling, found mainly in Alaska, the Yukon and the Northwest Territories, and whitefish, which are widely distributed in the northern states and Canada but have minor importance to anglers.

For the purposes of this book, the term "trout" includes not only true trout (genus *Salmo* and *Oncorhynchus*), but also chars (genus *Salvelinus*). True trout, such as browns and rainbows, have dark spots on a light background. Chars, such as brook trout and Dolly Varden, have light spots on a dark background. Chars require colder water than true trout.

Atlantic salmon are closely related to brown trout and belong to the same genus, Salmo. Pacific salmon (genus *Oncorhynchus*) are more closely related to the other true trout. Pacific salmon spawn only once, dying soon afterward; other members of the family may live to spawn several times. All salmon species are anadromous; they spend their lives at sea, then return to freshwater streams to spawn. Salmon stocked in freshwater lakes spawn in lake tributaries.

Many species of trout, including rainbow, brook, brown and cut-throat, have anadromous forms with a different appearance than the forms limited to fresh water. The anadromous forms are generally sleeker and more silvery.

Powerful fighters, trout and salmon have remarkable stamina. Some species, like rainbow trout and Atlantic salmon, leap repeatedly when hooked; others, like brook trout, wage a deep, bulldog-style battle.

Most salmonids are excellent eating, but the trend is toward catch-and-release fishing. In some heavily fished waters, catch-and-release is mandatory. This practice ensures that the fish remain in a stream long enough to spawn and produce "wild" progeny. The other alternative, frowned upon by most trout enthusiasts, is put-and-take stocking.

Identification Key to Major Salmonoid Groups

Start with the pair of pictures marked 1. It will identify the correct salmonoid group or send you to another pair of pictures.

1 DORSAL FIN *longer than head (left)* ....GRAYLING
Dorsal fin shorter than head (right) ....*go to 2*

2 ANAL FIN *longer than deep (left)* ....
PACIFIC SALMON

Anal fin no longer than deep (right) ....
go to 3

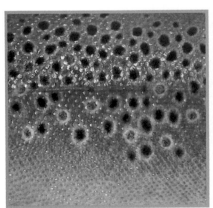 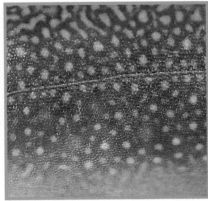

3 DARK SPOTS *on light background (left)* ......
TROUT AND ATLANTIC SALMON

Light spots on dark background (right) ....
CHARS

TROUT

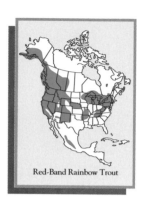

Red-Band Rainbow Trout

RED-BAND RAINBOW TROUT (*Oncorhynchus mykiss gairdneri*).
All rainbows have radiating rows of black spots on tail, black spots on back and sides, and no teeth on tongue. Common rainbows have pinkish horizontal band and pinkish gill cover with some black spots. Fly rod world record: 28 lbs.; Skeena River, British Columbia; 1985.

Steelhead

STEELHEAD (*Oncorhynchus mykiss irideus*).
Body longer and sleeker than that of common rainbow; fewer spots below lateral line. Steelhead may have faint pinkish horizontal band and gill cover, but gill cover has few or no black spots. All-tackle world record: 42 lbs., 2 oz.; Bell Island, Alaska; 1970.

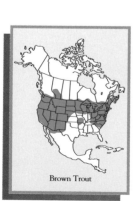

Brown Trout

BROWN TROUT (*Salmo trutta*).
Square tail with few or no spots; adipose fin (arrow) with some spots. Sides light brownish to yellowish with black spots and usually some red or orange spots. Spots often have whitish to bluish halos. Fly rod world record: 29 lbs, 12 oz.; Rio Grande River, Tierra del Fuego, Argentina; 1992.

Yellowstone Cutthroat Trout

YELLOWSTONE CUTTHROAT TROUT

(Oncorhynchus clarki bouvieri). All cutthroat have reddish slash marks on throat, black spots on tail, and patch of teeth at base of tongue. Yellowstones have spots above and below lateral line; spots are more concentrated toward rear. No official record.

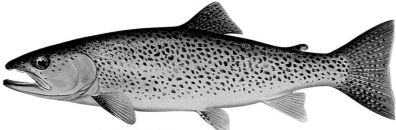

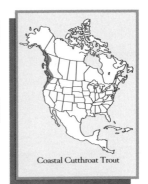

Coastal Cutthroat Trout

COASTAL CUTTHROAT TROUT

(Oncorhynchus clarki clarki). Sides and back heavily spotted; spots uniformly distributed from front to rear. Background color more silvery than that of other subspecies of cut-throat, and reddish slash marks on throat may be faint. No official record.

West Slope Cutthroat Trout

WEST SLOPE CUTTHROAT TROUT

(Oncorhynchus clarki lewisi). Spots on West Slope cutthroat are even more concentrated toward rear than those on Yellowstone cutthroat. But the spots are somewhat smaller and usually absent on front half of body below lateral line. No official record.

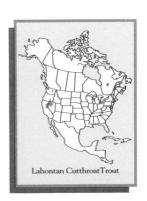

Lahontan CutthroatTrout

LAHONTAN CUTTHROAT TROUT

(Oncorhynchus clarki henshawi). Spotting relatively uniform. Spots widely spaced with some larger than the pupil. This is the largest form of cutthroat. Found mainly in western lakes. Fly rod world record: 14 lbs., 1 oz.; Pyramid Lake, Nevada; 1982.

TROUT (cont.) AND GRAYLING

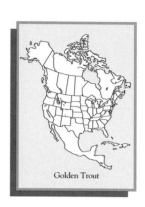

Golden Trout

GOLDEN TROUT (*Oncorhynchus aguabonita*).
Golden sides with reddish horizontal band that runs through about 10 dusky, oval-shaped marks. Tail spotted. Dorsal, pelvic and anal fins with white tips. Fly rod world record: 5 lbs; Golden Lake, Wyoming; 1989.

Arctic Grayling

ARCTIC GRAYLING (*Thymallus articus*).
Dorsal fin with base at least as long as fish's head; fin has rows of blue or violet spots. Pelvic fins with light streaks. Sides violet-gray and silver with small dark spots. Fly rod world record: 3 lbs., 10 oz.; Kazan River, N.W.T; 1989.

CHARS

Brook Trout

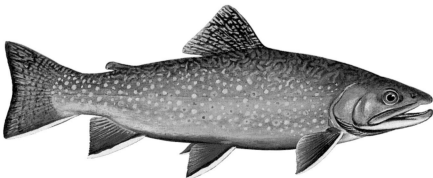

BROOK TROUT (*Salvelinus fontinalis*).
Background color brownish to greenish. Back laced with light, wormlike marks; sides have light spots and some red spots, both with blue halos. Lower fins with white leading edges. Fly rod world record: 10 lbs., 7 oz.; Assinica Broadback River, Quebec; 1982.

Lake Trout

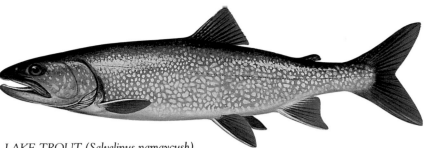

LAKE TROUT (*Salvelinus namaycush*).
Deeply forked tail; light spots on a background varying from light green or gray, to dark green, brown or black. Light spots cover the head. Lower fins with white leading edges. Fly rod world record: 27 lbs., 8 oz.; Nueltin Lake, Manitoba; 1994.

Arctic Char

ARCTIC CHAR (*Salvelinus alpinus*).
Background color silvery green. Sides with pinkish, reddish or cream-colored spots, some at least as large as pupil of eye. Lower fins with white leading edges. Fly rod world record: 20 lbs., 4 oz.; Tree River, N.W.T.; 1993.

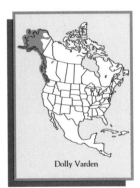

Dolly Varden

DOLLY VARDEN (*Salvelinus malma*).
Silvery green sides with pinkish, reddish or whitish spots. Lower fins with white leading edges. Resembles Arctic char and bull trout, but spots smaller than char's, and head less flattened than bull's. Fly rod world record: 12 lbs., 12 oz.; Wiluk River, Alaska; 1992.

BULL TROUT (*Salvelinus confluentus*).
Sides silvery green to dark green with pinkish to whitish spots. Lower fins with white leading edges. Head considerably longer, broader and more flattened than that of Dolly Varden. Fly rod world record: 11 lbs., 14 oz.; Flathead River, Montana; 1991.

Bull Trout

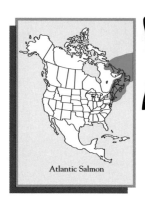

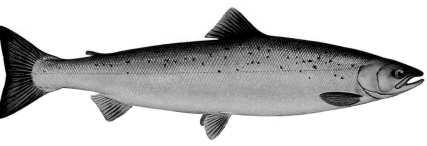

Atlantic Salmon

ATLANTIC SALMON *(Salmo salar)*.
Sides silvery to yellowish brown. Like brown trout, Atlantic salmon have few or no spots on tail. Tail slightly forked rather than square. Adipose fin unspotted; adipose of brown spotted. Fly rod world record: 51 lbs., 2 oz.; Alta River, Norway; 1994.

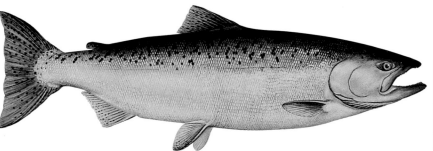

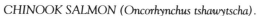

CHINOOK SALMON *(Oncorhynchus tshawytscha)*.
Also called king salmon. Sides silvery; upper sides, back and lobes of tail peppered with small black spots. Teeth set in blackish gums. Anal fin, usually with 15 to 19 rays, is longer than that of other Pacific salmon. Fly rod world record: 63 pounds; Trask River, Oregon; 1987.

Chinook Salmon

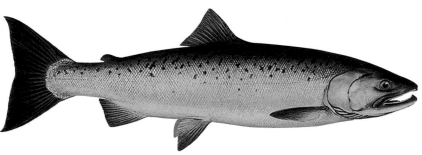

Coho Salmon

COHO SALMON *(Oncorhynchus kisutch)*. *Also called silver salmon. Resembles chinook, but tail has small black spots on upper lobe only. Teeth set in whitish to grayish gums. Anal fin considerably shorter than that of chinook, usually with 12 to 15 rays. Fly rod world record: 21 pounds; Karluk River, Kodiak Island, Alaska; 1988.*

Pink Salmon

PINK SALMON (*Oncorhynchus gorbuscha*).
Also called humpback salmon because of spawning male's distinct hump. Sides silvery; upper sides, back and entire tail with large black spots, some as large as eye. Spots on back, sides and tail of chinook much smaller than eye. Fly rod world record: 11 lbs., 8 oz.; Karluk River, Kodiak Island, Alaska; 1984.

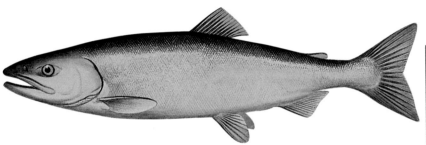

Sockeye Salmon

SOCKEYE SALMON (*Oncorhynchus nerka*).
Also called red salmon because of spawning color. Silvery sides with brilliant bluish to greenish back, often with black speckles. Tail unspotted. Resembles chum salmon, but lacks the faint vertical bands. Fly rod world record: 14 lbs., 8 oz.; Mulchatna River, Alaska; 1993.

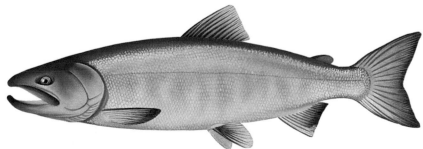

Chum Salmon

CHUM SALMON (*Oncorhynchus keta*).
Also called dog salmon because of its inferior eating quality. Sides silvery, often with black speckles on the back but no distinct black spots. Faint vertical bands on the side intensify as spawning time nears. Fly rod world record: 23 lbs., 14 oz.; Stillaguamish River, Washington; 1985.

Senses

Trout depend mainly on visual signals to detect danger. Any quick movement, heavy footstep or shadow will immediately put them down. But trout also have an excellent sense of smell and a well-developed lateral-line sense.

VISION. When approaching trout, remember that they see above-water objects through a window, a circular area on the surface whose size depends on the depth of the fish. The diameter is slightly more than twice as wide as the fish is deep. A trout at a depth of 2 feet

TROUT view the outside world through a window on the water's surface.

would have a window 4 feet, 6 inches wide. Surrounding the window, the surface is a mirror, through which the fish cannot see out.

Most light rays entering the window are bent, so the above-water field of vision is larger than you would expect. Rays near the edge of the window are bent and compressed most, so objects at a low angle are highly distorted. If you stay low enough, less than 10 degrees above the edge of the window, you will be completely hidden from the fish's view.

Trout and salmon have only fair night vision. With the exception of large brown trout, they do very little feeding after dark. And even browns seem to have difficulty locating a fly unless it produces noise or vibration.

SMELL. Trout and salmon use their sense of smell to find food, avoid predators and locate spawning areas. If you drop a gob of fresh salmon eggs in a clear pond filled with rainbows, the eggs will "milk" as they sink, leaving a scent trail. Feeding trout mill about until they cross the trail, then they turn and follow it to the eggs.

Researchers in British Columbia found that salmon turned back from their spawning run and headed downstream when a bear was fishing upstream of them. The salmon detected a chemical emitted by the bear called L-serine. This chemical is also given off by human skin.

Salmon and migratory forms of trout navigate at sea or in large lakes using the sun, currents and the earth's magnetic field. These clues enable them to return to the vicinity of their home stream at spawning time. Once they get this far, they rely on scent to find the right stream. Amazingly, they can return to the exact area of the stream where their life began. When researchers cut a salmon's olfactory nerves, it could not find its way back.

LATERAL LINE. Veteran fishermen step lightly when wading the streambed or walking the bank, even when outside the fish's field of vision. And they know that large, vibration-producing flies work best in murky water or after dark. The fish detect the footsteps and vibrations from the fly with their lateral-line system, a network of ultra-sensitive nerve endings along the side of the body.

Use small-diameter tippets when drifting a dry fly over the trout's window of vision. Apply leader-sink compound to the end of the tippet to make it sink beneath the surface. This reduces the leader's visibility. Knotless leaders also minimize visibility. Because there are no knots, these leaders are less affected by the current, so they produce less drag. And they will not catch as much floating debris as knotted leaders.

Feeding & Growth

Young trout and salmon rely heavily on aquatic insects for food. They feed mainly on immature forms, but may take some adults. They also eat terrestrial insects, small crustaceans, mollusks and earthworms.

As the fish grow larger, they continue to eat a lot of insects, but small fish make up an increasing percentage of their diet. Large trout do not hesitate to eat small animals like frogs and mice. Some salmon species, such as sockeye and pink, are plankton feeders, filtering tiny organisms from the water with their closely spaced gill rakers. This feeding behavior makes them difficult to catch on hook and line. Practically all trout and salmon will eat the eggs and young of other species, and of their own kind, when the opportunity presents itself.

How fast a trout grows depends not only on the type of food it eats, but also on the fertility and size of the lake or stream.

Trout that feed primarily on insects grow more slowly than those that eat lots of small fish; insect feeding consumes more energy for the amount of nutrients obtained. Trout in mountain streams usually grow slower than those in farm-country streams. These high-altitude streams are colder and less fertile, so they produce considerably less food.

Trout that live in small brooks or ponds usually have a slower growth rate than those in good-sized rivers or lakes because the bigger water offers a greater abundance and diversity of foods.

Genetics also affects growth rate. Fast-growing strains of many species have evolved naturally or have been produced by fish culturists who select and breed the fastest-growing individuals from each year-class.

Male trout and salmon grow faster than females; salmonids differ in this respect from most other fish species.

NIGHT STALKING FOR BROWNS

The best way to catch big brown trout is to fish at night, using large flies and aggressive retrieves that appeal to their lateral-line sense. Work large streamer patterns (minnow or crayfish imitations) along undercut stream banks, using split shot to get down. Retrieve with strong twitches to draw strikes from fish that seldom show themselves during daylight hours.

Spawning

GREAT CHANGES IN STORE

Before spawning, trout and salmon undergo astounding anatomical changes. A male's jaws lengthen and the lower jaw develops a large hook, or kype. The teeth of male Pacific salmon grow much larger before spawning, evidently to help them defend their territories.

Male pinks and sockeyes develop a pronounced hump on the back, ahead of the dorsal fin. Their grotesque appearance may intimidate predators and competing males that approach the spawning site.

Both sexes undergo dramatic color shifts, which are different for different species. In most cases, colors become darker and more intense. The changes are most pronounced in Pacific salmon. As spawning time approaches and their bodies begin to deteriorate, they change from bright silver to brilliant red, olive green or even black.

Most salmonids spawn in fall, but some, like the rainbow trout, spawn in the spring. Trout, char, grayling and Atlantic salmon live to spawn several times, but Pacific salmon spawn only once, then die. Typically, salmonids require flowing water to spawn, but brook trout and sockeye salmon sometimes spawn in lakes. All but the grayling dig a redd, or nest, for depositing eggs. Spawning habits of salmonids are summarized in the chart on page 25.

SPAWNING SITE. Trout and salmon prefer a clean gravel bottom for spawning, usually at the tail of a pool or in some other area where the current sweeps the bottom free of silt. The female digs the redd. She turns on her side and beats her tail against the bottom, moving the gravel away and creating a depression longer than her body and about half as deep.

As the female digs, she is often accompanied by more than one male; the largest male is dominant and defends his territory by charging the smaller ones, using his kype to nip them. A female commonly digs several redds, depositing a portion of her eggs in each.

SPAWNING ACT. The dominant male courts the female by nudging and quivering. Finally, the two lie side by side in the redd. They become rigid, arch their backs, and with their mouths agape, vibrate to release sperm and eggs. Sometimes, the other males also deposit sperm in the redd.

After spawning, the female digs at the upstream edge of the redd, covering the eggs with several inches of gravel. When all spawning activity is completed, the parents abandon the redd. Salmonids do not attempt to guard the young after they hatch.

EGGS AND INCUBATION. Trout and salmon are less prolific than most other gamefish. They have very large eggs, few in number. A 10-pound rainbow deposits only about 4,000 eggs; a walleye of the

SALMON often wiggle upstream through inches of water to reach their spawning grounds.

same size, for comparison, about 200,000. Salmonid eggs incubate from 1 to 5 months, depending on species. This long incubation period subjects the eggs to many hazards, such as disease and flooding. Eggs that are not well buried are quickly eaten by predators such as crayfish, insects and fish, including trout.

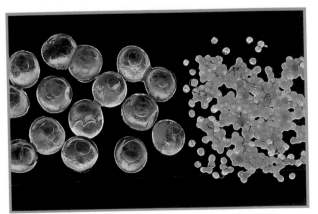

SALMON EGGS
(left) vs. walleye eggs.

JUVENILE STAGES. The eggs hatch in the gravel, and at first the fry can move very little. They do not feed, but get nutrients from the attached yolk sac. After several

FRY *with attached yolk sacs.*

weeks, they gain enough strength to wiggle through the gravel and emerge into the stream. Soon afterward, the fry absorb the yolk sac and begin feeding on plankton.

As the fish grow, they develop a row of dark, oval-shaped marks along the side. At this stage, the fish are called *parr*; the markings, *parr marks*. All species of trout and salmon, except the golden trout, lose their parr marks as they mature.

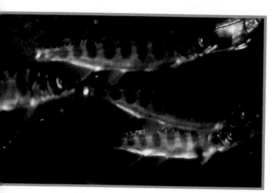

PARR

In the case of anadromous fishes like salmon and steelhead, the young spend at least 6 months, and sometimes as long as 3 years, in the home stream before they start to develop migratory tendencies. Then, the parr marks disappear, the sides turn a brilliant silver and the fish begin moving downstream. This process is called *smolting*, and the young are called *smolts*. The smolts spend several years at sea or in a large lake before reaching maturity.

Predation is severe during a trout's early life. Kingfishers, herons, otters and fish take the greatest toll. As a rule, fewer than 1 percent of newly hatched fry survive to age 1.

SMOLTS

Species	Spawning Temp. (°F)	Time of Year	Typical Spawning Site	Other
Rainbow trout	50-60	Spring	Small tributary	Steelhead spawns in tail of pool in swift stream
Brown trout	44-48	Fall	Upper portion of stream or small tributary	
Cutthroat trout	43-47	Spring	Smallest tributary	Some populations spawn only in alternate years
Golden trout	48-52	Mid-summer	Tails of pools in main stream or tributary	
Brook trout	40-49	Early fall	Headwaters of stream	May spawn around springs in lakes
Bull trout	45-50	Early fall	Small tributary	
Dolly Varden	40-45	Fall	Main channel	Eggs must incubate in very cold water
Arctic char	37-41	Fall	Quiet pool, usually below falls	
Arctic grayling	44-50	Early spring	Small tributary	Does not build a redd
Pink salmon	43-48	Fall	Lower portion of river	Runs are heavier in alternate years
Chinook salmon	40-55	Fall	Deep riffles in main channel	Separate runs in spring, summer and fall
Coho salmon	46-52	Late fall	Slow-moving tributary or slough	
Chum salmon	45-55	Fall	Small, slow-moving tributary	
Sockeye salmon	45-52	Fall	Tributaries of upstream lakes	May spawn along lakeshore
Atlantic salmon	42-50	Fall	Upper portion of large river system	Leaps seemingly impassable falls

Habitat

GOOD trout streams have a rocky bottom, moderate current and a riffle-run-pool configuration.

Compared to most warmwater fish species, which will tolerate a broad range of environmental conditions, salmonids have more specific habitat requirements.

WATER TEMPERATURE. Trout and salmon are classified as *cold-water* species. Whether they live in lakes or streams, they require cold water year-round. Lake trout and Arctic char prefer the coldest water, from 45° to 50°F; brown trout, the warmest, from 60° to 65°. Browns and rainbows are found in streams where summertime water temperatures may reach 80°F during low-flow periods. But at that temperature, they are under stress and do very little feeding. Surface temperatures in trout lakes may also reach the 80-degree mark in summer, but the fish can easily reach cooler water by going deeper, assuming the depths are well oxygenated.

MOST good trout lakes are deep, cold, clear and infertile.

DISSOLVED OXYGEN. Most kinds of trout and salmon require a dissolved oxygen level of about 5 parts per million. In streams, the constant mixing keeps oxygen levels higher than that. But in fertile lakes, oxygen levels in the depths may fall too low to support salmonids. Plankton in the water and decomposing organic material on the bottom consume too much of the available oxygen.

This explains why lakes of low fertilility are best suited to trout. Their clear water lacks the nutrients needed to produce heavy algal blooms, so oxygen is not consumed as fast.

WATER CLARITY. Trout and salmon are usually found in clear water, but they can tolerate waters of low clarity, as long as they have cool enough temperatures and adequate dissolved oxygen. Browns and rainbows are more tolerant of low-clarity water than other species.

STABILITY OF FLOW. A reliable year-round flow is a must for stream-dwelling salmonids. If the flow drops too low in summer, the water warms up too much, killing the fish. If it drops too low in winter, the stream may freeze to the bottom. Streams with plenty of spring flow are least likely to experience these problems.

27

Weather

RAINDROPS rippling the surface mean excellent trout fishing.

No matter if you fish in lakes or streams, weather has a major impact on trout and salmon fishing. As a rule, the fish are most active under low-light conditions, so overcast skies are better for fishing than sunny skies. In sunny weather, trout are extra-wary, seeking the cover of boulders, logs or undercut banks, or moving to deep water. In cloudy weather, they are more aggressive and more willing to leave cover to find food.

A moderate wind or light rain that ripples the surface reduces light penetration, so the fish bite better than they would if the surface were calm. The wind also makes the fish more aggressive. It blows insects into the water, causing trout to start feeding. But trout have difficulty spotting small insects when the surface is too choppy, so dry-fly fishing is not as effective as it would be if the water were calm. An intense wind or heavy rain pelting the surface usually puts the fish down.

Air temperature also has a dramatic influence on feeding activity. Insects may stop hatching for two or three days after a severe cold front. The effects of air temperature are more noticeable in streams than in lakes. Most trout and salmon feed heaviest at water temperatures from 55° to 60°F. On a typical stream, warm, sunny weather early or late in the season will drive the water temperature to that range by midafternoon, triggering an insect hatch and starting a feeding spree. But in summer, the same type of weather warms the water too much by midafternoon, so fishing is poor. Trout bite better in the morning or evening, when the water is cooler.

Rain also has more effect on stream fishing, because it changes the clarity and level of the water, which largely determine where the fish will be found and how well they bite.

A light to moderate rain is ideal. It slightly clouds the water, washes terrestrial foods into the stream, and increases the flow, causing more immature aquatic insects to drift downstream. A prolonged downpour, on the other hand, muddies the water so much that the fish cannot see, and with the rising water, they abandon their normal locations. To make matters worse, the infusion of warm water from a summer rain may turn the fish off.

Rain also has a dramatic effect on anadromous trout and salmon. Fish entering a stream to spawn stage up at the stream mouth. A few enter the stream at normal flow, but the majority wait for the increased flow resulting from a heavy rain. Fishing is poor as long as the stream stays muddy, but improves rapidly when the water starts to clear.

MUGGY WEATHER MEANS MAYFLIES

Humid summer days often bring off heavy hatches of mayflies, particularly Tricos (tiny mayfly species) and Hexagenia (large mayfly species). When the Trico hatch is on, trout congregate in areas with slow current and lots of rooted vegetation to feed on the spinners, which fall to the water like snowflakes. Fish them with size 20-26 spentwing spinner imitations. Hexagenia mayflies hatch from mud-bottomed pools. Trout feed on the emerging nymphs as well as the spinners. Use size 2-6 mayfly nymphs or dry flies.

LARGEMOUTH BASS

Largemouth Bass Basics

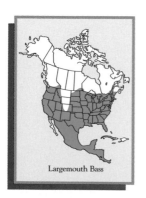

Largemouth Bass

Renowned for its explosive strikes and spectacular leaps, the largemouth bass is a favorite among millions of freshwater fishermen. Originally, largemouths were found only east of the Mississippi River and south of the Great Lakes. But as bass fishing grew in popularity, so did stocking programs in many states. Largemouth are now caught in waters throughout the continental United States and Hawaii, in addition to southern Canada and most of Mexico. Bass have been introduced in Europe, Asia, Africa, and South America.

The largemouth is the largest member of a group of closely related fishes called black bass. Others include the smallmouth, spotted, red-eye, Suwannee and Guadalupe. The largemouth is distinguished from all of these species by a jaw that extends beyond the eye. All black bass belong to the sunfish family, but differ from sunfish because of their longer bodies.

Largemouth range from deep green to pale olive across the back, with bellies that are a shade of white or yellow. They have a black lateral band that extends from head to tail.

Biologists have identified two subspecies of largemouth bass: the Florida largemouth and the northern largemouth. Originally, Florida bass lived only in Florida waters. Stocking efforts have expanded their range to include much of the South, particularly Texas and California.

Although they look alike, the Florida largemouth grows considerably larger than the northern subspecies. To be considered a real trophy, a Florida bass must weigh at least 12 pounds; a northern largemouth, only about 7.

Some biologists believe that the world-record largemouth bass was a cross between the northern and Florida subspecies. The 22-pound, 4-ounce largemouth was caught in Montgomery Lake, Georgia, in 1932. The fly rod world record weighed 13 pounds, 9 ounces and was caught in Lake Morena, California, in 1984.

*NOT ALL BASS
LOOK ALIKE*

Largemouth vary in color, depending upon the type of water. Bass from clear waters are dark; those from murky waters, pale.

The lateral band varies as well. It becomes more distinct when a fish is exposed to sunlight, but may disappear when the fish is in deep or murky water.

Lateral
Line

Senses

Largemouth bass possess the five major senses common to most animals: hearing, sight, smell, taste and touch. They also have a very well-developed lateral-line sense.

The lateral line, a series of sensitive nerve endings that extends from behind the gill to the tail, can pick up underwater vibrations as subtle as a swimming baitfish. In one experiment, researchers placed small cups over the eyes of bass, then dropped minnows into a tank with them. The bass ate each minnow, using their lateral lines to locate them. This explains how bass can detect a lure in the murkiest water.

Largemouth have ears located within the skull. They may be attracted by the gurgling noise of a popper, but when they hear loud, unfamiliar sounds, they usually swim to cover. Many bass fishermen carpet the bottoms of their boats to reduce noise that might spook the fish.

Bass can see in all directions, except directly below or behind. In clear water, they can see 30 feet or more. But in most bass waters, visibility is limited to 5 or 10 feet. Largemouth can also see objects that are above water. To avoid spooking fish in clear water, many fishermen wear neutral-colored clothing that blends into the background.

A largemouth's eye absorbs more light than does a human eye, enabling the fish to see food in dim light or darkness. Bass will feed any time of the day or night, but are less inclined to leave cover under bright conditions. Like most fish, they prefer shade. They find better ambush camouflage in shady spots or under low-light conditions.

Largemouth smell through nostrils, or *nares*, which are short passageways through which water is drawn and expelled without entering the throat. Like most fish, bass can detect minute amounts of scent in the water. However, they rely on scent less than sunfish, salmon or trout. The sense of taste is not particularly important to largemouth; they have few taste cells in their mouths.

SEEING RED

Bass in shallow water can detect colors, and studies have shown them to be especially fond of red. But the best colors vary, depending on light conditions, water clarity and water color. Color selection is less important in deep water because most colors appear as shades of gray.

Feeding & Growth

Newly hatched largemouth feed heavily on tiny crustaceans and other zooplankton. When young largemouth reach about 2 inches in length, they begin to eat insects and small fish, including smaller bass. Adult largemouth prey mostly on fish, but crayfish, frogs and insects are important foods in some waters.

Wherever they live, bass rank high in the aquatic food chain. A bass 10 inches or larger has few enemies and will eat almost anything it can swallow. Because of its large mouth and flexible stomach, a bass can eat prey nearly half its own length.

A largemouth inhales small foods, quickly opening its mouth to suck in water and the food. It then forces the water out the gills while it either swallows or rejects the object. Largemouth can expel food as quickly as they inhale it, so anglers must set the hook immediately. Bass usually grab large prey, then turn the food to swallow it headfirst.

As the water warms, the metabolism of bass increases and they feed more often. Largemouth seldom eat at water temperatures below 50°F. From 50° to 68°F, feeding increases, and from 68° to 80°F, they feed heavily. At temperatures above 80°F, however, feeding declines.

No one is certain what causes bass to strike artificial flies or other lures. Experts point to hunger as the main reason, but reflex, aggressiveness, curiosity and competitiveness may play a part.

Reflex, or a sudden instinctive reaction, explains why a bass with a full stomach strikes a popper the instant it hits the water. The fish has little time to judge what it is grabbing, yet some cue triggers it to strike.

Male bass display aggressiveness when they attack lures or chase other fish that invade their nest sites. Although this behavior is common during nesting season, bass are not as aggressive at other times of the year.

Curiosity may be the reason that bass rush up to inspect new objects or sounds. However, it is doubtful they take food solely out of curiosity. Often several bass race to devour a single food item, particularly in waters where food is in short supply.

The best trophy bass waters are those where the fish grow rapidly as a result of favorable temperatures and abundant food. Largemouth seldom reach large sizes in waters where they have become too abundant.

The amount bass grow in a year depends on the length of their growing season, or the number of days suitable for growth. The growing season in the South may last twice as long as it does in the North. Largemouth gain weight most quickly in water from 75° to 80°F. They do not grow in water colder than 50°F. Although bass in the South grow and mature faster, they rarely live as long as those in colder, northern lakes. In southern waters, bass occasionally reach 10 years of age; in northern waters, they may live as long as 15 years.

Female bass live longer than males, so they are more apt to reach trophy size. In one study, 30 percent of the females were 5 years or older, while only 9 percent of the male bass were 5 years or more.

By far the best time to fly-fish for largemouth bass is in spring, when warming water draws baitfish and other bass foods into shallow bays, creek arms, backwaters and boat channels. The biggest bass often go deep in midsummer, especially in clear lakes, and may be difficult to reach with flies. But they sometimes feed in shallow water in morning and evening or in windy, overcast weather.

Bass in murky lakes or streams, however, often stay shallow all summer and can be easily taken by fly-fishermen using big, noisy flies.

Spawning

THE BIGGEST LITTLE ENEMY?

Sunfish often prey on bass eggs or newly hatched fry. In waters with large sunfish populations, the panfish can seriously hamper bass reproduction. A sunfish school surrounds the nest, and while the male chases some away, others invade the nest and devour the eggs or fry.

In spring, when inshore waters reach about 60°F, largemouth swim onto spawning grounds in shallow bays, backwaters, channels and other areas protected from the wind. Spawning grounds usually have firm bottoms of sand, gravel, mud or rock. Bass seldom nest on silt.

Male bass may spend several days selecting nest sites, which are usually in 1 to 4 feet of water, but may be deeper if the water is clear. Most bass nest in pockets in bulrushes, water lilies or other weeds. Bass in open areas often select a nest site on the sunny side of a submerged log or boulder. Nests are seldom made where a male can see another nesting male. Consequently, beds are usually at least 30 feet apart, but may be closer if underwater objects prevent the males from seeing each other.

Spawning begins when the water reaches 63° to 68°F and the temperature remains within this range for several days. Cold fronts may cause water temperatures to drop, which interrupts and delays spawning. A female bass lays 2,000 to 7,000 eggs per pound of body weight. She may deposit all of her eggs in one nest or drop them at several different sites. After spawning, she recuperates in deep water and does not feed for two or three weeks.

Alone on the nest, the male hovers above the eggs, slowly fanning them to keep off silt and debris. He does not feed while guarding the eggs, but will attack other fish, or flies, that get too near.

Bass eggs hatch in only 2 days at 72°F, but take 5 days at 67°F. Cold weather following spawning will delay hatching. If the shallows drop to 50°F, the fry will not emerge for 13 days. At lower temperatures, the eggs fail to develop. A severe cold front sometimes causes males to abandon the nest, resulting in a complete loss of eggs or fry. From 2,000 to 12,000 eggs hatch from the typical nest. Of these, only 5 to 10 are likely to survive to reach 10 inches in length.

How Largemouth Bass Spawn

SPAWNING *occurs as the male and female move over the nest with their vents close together. The male bumps and nips the female, stimulating her to deposit the eggs. Then the male covers the eggs with his sperm, or milt.*

PREPARING *the nest, the male largemouth shakes its head and tail to sweep away bottom debris. The typical nest is a saucer-shaped depression about 2 to 3 feet in diameter, or twice the length of the male.*

NEST-GUARDING *is left to the male bass. After hatching, the tiny fry lie in the nest for 8 to 10 days. Once they are able to swim, the fry remain in a compact school, hovering beneath weeds or other overhead cover. As the fry grow larger, they spread over a wider area, but the male still protects them. The male abandons the fry when they reach about 1 inch in length. After that, he may eat any fry he encounters.*

Habitat

Although largemouth bass are one of the most adaptable of all gamefish, there are certain habitat requirements necessary for their survival.

TEMPERATURE. Largemouth prefer water temperatures in the range of 68° to 78°F. But temperature alone does not determine their location. They will abandon an area with ideal temperature to escape bright sunlight or to find food or cover. Largemouth cannot survive at temperatures above 98°.

OXYGEN. Largemouth require an oxygen level of at least 2 parts per million to survive, but in order to function normally, they need about 5 parts per million. All lakes have sufficient oxygen in the shallows. But in fertile lakes, those with a high level of nutrients, the depths may not have adequate oxygen. Fertile lakes produce large amounts of plankton. These tiny plants and animals eventually die and sink to bottom where they decompose. The decomposition process consumes huge amounts of oxygen, making the depths unsuitable for fish. Heavy algae blooms are a symptom of high water fertility.

In the North, fertile lakes may *winterkill*. Thick ice and snow cover block out sunlight, so plants can no longer produce oxygen. Decomposition continues, drawing all oxygen from even the shallowest water. Bass are one of the first to die in winterkill lakes.

In deep, clear waters, such as canyon reservoirs and strip pits, water fertility is usually low. The water contains ample oxygen from top to bottom, so bass can move wherever they want.

OVERHEAD COVER in shallow water provides shade and cooler temperatures, allowing bass to remain all summer (opposite). Weedy edges provide points of ambush where bass can dart out to capture smaller fish.

COVER. Largemouth require cover from the moment they hatch. Bass fry crowd into dense weed beds to escape predatory fish. Later in their lives, bass use weeds, rocks, flooded timber and brush, sunken logs and other objects for shade, shelter and ambush points.

STRUCTURE. Structure is the geologic makeup of the bottom. It may be a reef, point or any other place where the depth changes. It can also be a rock patch or any other place where the bottom material changes from one type to another. Largemouth use structure as a reference point to guide their daily movements.

Experienced bass fishermen know that largemouth relate strongly to structure and cover, but many have observed that they also relate to isolated objects or any kind of unusual feature in the environment that helps them "get their bearings." In a controlled location experiment, fisheries researchers discovered that largemouth bass will relate to anything different in their surroundings, even a black stripe painted on the side of a white tank (opposite).

LARGEMOUTH often relate to sharp drop-offs.

HOW BASS RELATE TO FEATURES IN THEIR ENVIRONMENT

A PLAIN WHITE TANK lacks features to which the bass can relate. Lighting is evenly distributed and sounds carefully controlled. The bass swim about aimlessly.

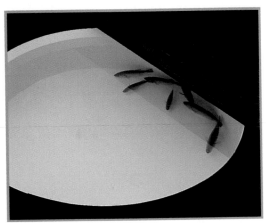

A BOARD over one edge of the tank provides acceptable cover for the bass. The fish station themselves in the shade under the board.

ROCKS piled in one area of the tank soon attract the bass. They form a closely packed school above and along the edge of the rock pile.

A BLACK STRIPE painted on the wall provides something to which bass can relate. They hover near the stripe, even though it offers no cover.

Weather

Weather plays a greater role in the daily activity of largemouth bass than any other factor. To improve your success, you should know how the following weather conditions affect bass fishing.

FRONTS. Largemouth feed heavily just before a strong cold front, often providing spectacular fishing for several hours. But once the front arrives, they eat very little until 1 or 2 days after the system passes. Catching bass under these conditions is difficult and may require smaller flies and a more delicate presentation.

Warm fronts affect bass in different ways, depending on the season and water temperatures. A series of warm days in spring or fall will raise water temperatures in the shallows, causing bass to feed.

In winter, several unusually warm days may draw bass toward the surface to absorb the warmth of the sun. The fish become more accessible to fishermen and more likely to feed or take a fly. But a string of hot days in summer may warm a shallow lake or pond so much that largemouth become sluggish and difficult to catch.

WIND. Wind can either improve or ruin fishing. A steady wind will concentrate minute organisms near shore or along timber and brush lines. Baitfish feed in these areas, attracting bass and other predators. In spring, warm winds blowing from the same direction for several days can pile up warm water on the downwind shore. This warmer water holds more bass than other areas of the lake.

Waves washing into shore create a band of muddy water. Bass hang along the mud line, where they can avoid bright light yet easily dart into clear water to grab food. The wind also pushes plankton toward shore, attracting baitfish, which, in turn, draw bass.

If the wind becomes too strong, it can impair fishing success in shallow areas. Turbulence caused by heavy waves pushes bass into deeper water, where they are harder to find. In shallow lakes, strong winds often churn the water enough to make the entire lake murky, slowing fishing for several days.

RAIN. Rainy weather usually improves bass fishing. Overcast skies reduce light penetration, so largemouth are more comfortable in shallow water. In reservoirs, runoff from tributaries flows into the back ends of creek arms. The murky water causes bass to move in and feed. The same situation occurs near stream inlets on many natural lakes.

Fishing success may decline during and after heavy rains. Runoff from torrential rains can muddy an entire body of water, causing fish to stop biting. Angling remains slow until the water clears, which may take several days or weeks.

Experienced fishermen can identify certain clouds and other atmospheric conditions that signal changes in the weather. They know how bass react to these changes and plan their angling strategy accordingly. Some of these indicators are described on the following pages.

Veteran bass fishermen love stable weather. When conditions are stable or changing very slowly, bass go through a routine of feeding and resting that is often predictable from one day to the next. For example, during an extended period of overcast weather, a school of bass may feed on a sharp breakline in midday, then drop back into deeper water. The school usually repeats this daily pattern, as long as weather conditions remain stable.

How a Cold Front Affects Bass Fishing

CIRRUS CLOUDS *usually precede a major cold front. These clouds may be 100 miles ahead of an approaching front. They indicate that largemouth will soon be feeding heavily.*

THUNDERHEADS *build as a front approaches. Lightning and strong winds often accompany these towering clouds. The feeding frenzy usually peaks just before these clouds arrive.*

CLEAR SKY *following a cold front filters out few of the sun's rays. Light penetrates deeper into the water, forcing bass to move out of the shallows.*

CUMULUS CLOUDS *promise better fishing. The white, fluffy clouds signal that the front has passed. Bass will soon resume their normal activity.*

How Wind and Rain Affect Bass Fishing

CALM conditions (left) enable bass in clear water to see objects above them. Fishermen and boaters easily spook bass in shallow water. But light wave action (right) or disturbance caused by raindrops refracts the light rays enough to make it more difficult for largemouth to see objects on or above the surface.

HEAVY RUNOFF into clear lakes creates patches of muddy water. Bass congregate wherever turbid water enters the lake, such as the inlets of streams and drainage ditches, or near storm sewer pipes.

LIGHTNING and thunder drive largemouth into the depths. If the weather looks threatening, head for shore immediately. Your boat may be the highest point on the lake, making you vulnerable to a lightning strike.

SMALLMOUTH BASS

Smallmouth Bass Basics

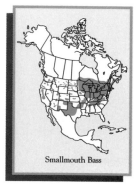

Smallmouth Bass

Known for its aerial acrobatics and never-give-up determination, the smallmouth bass has a well-deserved reputation as the fightingest freshwater gamefish. After a smallmouth strikes, it usually makes a sizzling run for the surface, does several cartwheels in an attempt to throw the fly, then wages a dogged battle in deep water.

The smallmouth bass, *Micropterus dolomieui*, was originally found mainly in the eastern United States. Its range extended from northern Minnesota to southern Quebec on the north, and from northern Georgia to eastern Oklahoma on the south. It was not found east of

SMALLMOUTH BASS have 9 dark vertical bars that come and go, and 3 bars radiating from the eye. They lack the dark horizontal band present on largemouth bass, and normally have a darker belly. Smallmouth have a chameleonlike ability to change color to match their surroundings.

the Appalachians. But due to its tremendous popularity, the smallmouth has been widely stocked and is now found in every state with the exception of Florida, Louisiana and Alaska. It has also been stocked in most Canadian provinces and in Asia, Africa, Europe and South America.

The smallmouth is sometimes called bronzeback because of the bronze reflections from its scales. Other common names include black bass, brown bass, Oswego bass, redeye and green trout.

Like its close relatives the largemouth and spotted bass, the smallmouth belongs to the sunfish family. Smallmouth have been known to hybridize naturally with spotted bass, and biologists have created a smallmouth-largemouth hybrid nicknamed the "meanmouth" because of its aggressive nature.

Although smallmouth bass are considered good eating, the modern trend in sport fishing is toward catch-and-release, especially in heavily fished waters. Where fishing pressure is heavy, the large smallmouth are quickly removed, leaving only the small ones.

The largest smallmouth bass ever taken on a fly rod weighed 6 pounds, 4 ounces. It was caught in Pine Lake, Michigan, in 1995.

HOW TO DISTINGUISH SMALLMOUTH BASS FROM LARGEMOUTH BASS

Basswood Lake, Ont. (slightly bog stained)

Lake George, N.Y. (very clear)

MOUTH SIZE *clearly separates smallmouth bass (top) from largemouth bass (bottom). On a smallmouth, the upper jaw extends to the middle of the eye; on a largemouth, beyond the rear of the eye.*

Percy Priest Lake, Tenn. (greenish)

COLOR PHASE *of smallmouth bass varies greatly in different waters, depending mainly on the color of the water. These photos show three of the many possible color phases.*

Senses

To find food and escape danger, smallmouth rely on eyesight to a far greater degree than any of their other senses. As a result, good smallmouth fishermen generally use flies with a natural look. And they take great pains to avoid being seen by the smallmouth, especially when fishing in clear water.

Little scientific research has been done on the smallmouth's sensory capabilities, but some conclusions can be drawn based on field observation. For instance, smallmouth evidently have a well-developed lateral-line sense because they can detect flies that produce vibration in water where the visibility is only a few inches. They also have good hearing as evidenced by the fact that they are easily spooked by noise, especially noise that is transmitted directly into the water. Experienced small-

SENSES OF SMALLMOUTH BASS VS. THOSE OF OTHER GAMEFISH*

Fish Species	Daytime Vision	Night Vision	Lateral Line	Smell	Hearing
Smallmouth Bass	Excellent	Good	Good	Fair	Good
Largemouth Bass	Good	Fair	Good	Fair	Good
Northern Pike	Excellent	Poor	Good	Poor	Good
Crappie	Good	Good	Fair	Fair	Fair
Bluegill	Excellent	Fair	Fair	Good	Fair
Trout	Excellent	Good	Excellent	Excellent	Good

Ratings determined from a survey of fish physiologists and fisheries biologists.

mouth fishermen are careful not to drop the anchor on the floor of the boat or create excess disturbance while wading.

The sense of smell apparently plays some role in extremely turbid water, but in most situations it appears to be less important than the other senses.

Studies have shown that smallmouth bass are less line- and lure-wary than largemouth bass, and thus easier to catch. But the degree of wariness varies greatly in different waters, depending mainly on the amount of competition for food. In waters where the smallmouth population is low and food plentiful, smallmouth can be extremely cautious. Any sudden movement by a fisherman will scare them into deeper water, where they refuse to bite. The best policy is to keep a low profile and avoid throwing your shadow over the fish.

But if the population is high and food relatively scarce, smallmouth are not as wary. In fact, scuba divers have attracted smallmouth to within a few feet by tapping rocks on their air tanks.

Habitat

Smallmouth bass are fish of clear, clean waters. They are equally at home in streams and lakes, but are rarely found in small ponds, lakes shallower than 25 feet, or any water that is continuously murky or polluted. To locate smallmouth, you should become familiar with their preferences in regard to the following environmental conditions:

TEMPERATURE. During the summer months, smallmouth in northern lakes are usually found at water temperatures from 67° to 71°F and seldom at temperatures above 80°. But smallmouth in southern reservoirs are often found at temperatures of 78° to 84°. This difference can be explained by the fact that the deeper, cooler water in the reservoirs lacks sufficient oxygen in summer.

Laboratory experiments have shown that smallmouth bass prefer a water temperature of approximately 82°F. But the majority of these experiments were conducted using juvenile smallmouth, whose temperature preference is considerably higher than that of the adult bass.

These findings have great significance for smallmouth fishermen. If you are fishing in shallow water and catching nothing but undersized smallmouth, you may be able to catch bigger ones by fishing several feet deeper, where the water is cooler.

During the cold months, activity of smallmouth bass drops off. In laboratory studies, smallmouth fed very little at temperatures below 50°F and lay motionless on the bottom at temperatures below 40°. In their natural surroundings, smallmouth respond to temperature in much the same way.

TEMPERATURE PREFERENCES AND OXYGEN REQUIREMENTS OF VARIOUS FRESHWATER FISH

Fish Species	Preferred Water Temperature (°F)	Oxygen Needs (parts per million)
Smallmouth Bass	67-71	2.5
Largemouth Bass	68-78	2.0
Bluegill	75-80	3.5
Northern Pike under 7 pounds over 7 pounds	65-70 50-55	1.4
Brook Trout	52-56	5.0
Black Bullhead	78-84	less than 1

OXYGEN. Smallmouth can tolerate an oxygen level of 2.5 parts per million, while largemouth can survive at 2.0. This slight difference may explain why largemouth are better able to tolerate stagnant water. But neither species fares well at oxygen levels this low. Feeding and growth are severely reduced if the level remains below 5 parts per million for an extended period.

In most smallmouth waters, the oxygen level is adequate throughout the depths that smallmouth prefer. So measuring the oxygen level will not help you locate the fish. But in highly fertile waters, smallmouth may be confined to shallow water in summer because the depths lack sufficient oxygen.

pH. Smallmouth are found in waters with a pH from 5 to 9. Although the best smallmouth populations are usually found where the pH is from 7.9 to 8.1, there is no research to indicate that smallmouth prefer any specific pH level. Canadian researchers found that smallmouth were unable to successfully reproduce at pH levels from 5.5 to 6.0.

CURRENT. Smallmouth prefer moderate current, usually in the range of 0.4 to 1.3 feet per second. This range is slower than that preferred by trout, but faster than that favored by largemouth bass. With a little experience, you will be able to recognize the right current speed. In most streams, smallmouth are more numerous in pools with noticeable current than in pools with slack water.

In lakes, smallmouth often concentrate around river mouths or in areas with wind-induced current, such as a trough between two islands or a narrow channel between two major lobes of a lake.

DEPTH. Smallmouth are generally considered fish of the *epilimnion*, the upper layer of water in a lake that is stratified into temperature layers. They are most likely to be found in shallow areas adjacent to deep water. The depths offer smallmouth refuge from intense light and boat traffic.

In waters with both smallmouth and largemouth, the smallmouth are usually slightly deeper. In spring, summer and early fall, smallmouth are seldom found at depths exceeding 30 feet. But in late fall and winter, you may find them in tight schools at depths down to 60 feet.

CLARITY. Although smallmouth will tolerate murky water for short periods, they rarely live in water that remains murky year-round. As a rule, waters where the visibility is less than 1 foot do not hold substantial smallmouth populations.

If the water is murky in one portion of a lake but clear in another, chances are that smallmouth will be most numerous in the clearer area. Similarly, smallmouth are usually more plentiful in a clear reach of a stream than in a muddy reach. And in extremely fertile lakes, smallmouth bite best in spring, before intense algae blooms cloud the water, and in fall, after the algae has died back.

BOTTOM TYPE. In most waters, smallmouth are found over a bottom consisting of clean rocks or gravel. This type of bottom is usually rich in smallmouth foods including crayfish and larval insects like dragonfly nymphs and hellgrammites. But in lakes where most of the basin consists of rock, smallmouth often prefer sandy shoal areas, especially those with a sparse growth of weeds. The sandy, weedy areas will hold fewer crayfish and insect larvae, but more baitfish.

Other species that compete with smallmouth for food, living space or spawning habitat can greatly affect the size of the smallmouth population and the way smallmouth behave. Compared to most other gamefish, smallmouth are poor competitors. If a body of water contains numerous shallow-water predators, like largemouth bass or northern pike, chances are it will not support a dense smallmouth population.

Competition also affects smallmouth location. Most reservoirs in the mid-South, for example, have good largemouth populations. In these waters, largemouth tend to dominate the upper reaches, where the water is shallower and the clarity lower. They also thrive in weedy or brushy creek arms. Smallmouth are found in the main-lake area, where the water is deep and clear. In reservoirs with fewer largemouth, smallmouth may occupy the upper as well as the lower reaches.

Feeding & Growth

If you have ever caught a smallmouth and examined its stomach contents, chances are you found bits and pieces of crayfish. In waters where crayfish are plentiful, they make up at least two-thirds of the smallmouth's diet.

Because crayfish inhabit the same rocky areas that smallmouth do, they make a convenient target for feeding bass. Other important items in the smallmouth's diet include fish, adult and immature insects and tadpoles.

The diet of smallmouth bass may vary from season to season, depending on the availability of food. In a 5-year food habits study conducted on Nebish Lake, Wisconsin, crayfish made up 83 percent of the

GROWTH RATES OF SMALLMOUTH BASS AT VARIOUS LATITUDES

Lake Name and Latitude	Age 1	2	3	4	5	6	7	8	9	10
		Length in Inches at Various Ages								
Lake Opeongo, Ont. (46°N)	2.1	5.2	7.7	9.1	11.1	12.1	13.5	14.5	15.5	–
Northern Lake Michigan (45°N)	3.9	6.3	8.1	9.7	11.5	13.2	14.6	15.8	16.8	17.4
Lake Sincoe, Ont. (44°N)	4.2	6.3	8.6	10.9	13.0	14.6	15.8	16.9	17.0	–
Quabbin Lake, Mass. (42.5°N)	3.5	6.7	10.2	12.9	14.7	16.1	16.7	17.1	17.3	17.5
Pine Flat Lake, Cal. (37°N)	5.5	8.9	12.5	14.7	16.6	17.9	18.3	–	–	–
Norris Lake, Tenn. (36°N)	3.1	8.9	13.3	15.8	17.4	18.0	18.6	20.9	–	–
Pickwick Lake, Ala. (35°N)	5.9	10.7	13.5	16.6	18.5	20.4	21.0	21.6	–	–

smallmouth's diet in September, but only 14 percent in May. The diet contained 34 percent insects in May, but only 4 percent in July.

Smallmouth feed very little during cold-water periods. Normally, they begin feeding in spring when the water temperature reaches the upper 40s. Food consumption peaks at water temperatures around 78°F. When the water temperature drops below 40°, practically no feeding takes place.

Smallmouth bass differ from most other freshwater gamefish in that the males and females grow at about the same rate. Smallmouth in lakes and reservoirs usually grow faster and reach a larger size than those in streams. And smallmouth in the South generally grow faster than those in the North (table above), although growth rates vary less than might be expected. Smallmouth weighing up to 11 pounds, 8 ounces have been taken in Canadian waters.

Smallmouth live as long as 18 years in the North, but seldom longer than 7 years in the South, where higher metabolic rates cause faster burnout. The table above shows how growth rates vary.

THINK LOW FOR RIVER SMALLIES

The best time to fly-fish for river smallmouth is in late summer, when the water level drops very low and confines smallmouth to the deepest pools. With so many fish concentrated in a small area, a food shortage often develops, causing smallmouth to become very agggressive. Try crayfish or leech patterns, zonkers, stonefly imitations or poppers.

Spawning

TO FISH OR NOT TO FISH

The practice of fishing for smallmouth on the spawning beds is highly controversial. Even if the fish are released, many anglers feel that the practice is detrimental.

The male guards the fry on the nest for 5 to 7 days and usually continues to guard them for another week or two after the school leaves the nest.

If fisherman catch the guarding male, panfish may quickly consume the eggs or fry. In one study, a single bluegill ate 39 smallmouth fry when the male was momentarily driven away. Wading anglers may also damage the nest by stepping on it.

Smallmouth can spawn successfully in lakes or streams. A typical spawning site is near an object like a rock or log which shelters it from strong current or wave action. Such an object also makes it easier for a male to guard the nest because predators cannot sneak in from behind. Nests are usually in water 2 to 4 feet deep, although they have been found in water as deep as 20 feet. Smallmouth almost always nest on sand, gravel or rubble and avoid mud bottoms.

Males begin building nests in spring, when the water temperature stabilizes above 55°F. A male uses his tail to fan out a circular nest with a diameter about twice as great as his own length. On a rubble bottom, he simply sweeps debris off the rocks. On a sand or gravel bottom, he fans out a depression from 2 to 4 inches deep. A male nests in the same vicinity each year and will sometimes use the same nest.

Females move into the nesting area a few days later. When a male spots a female, he rushes toward her and attempts to drive her to the nest. At first, she swims away, but she returns again later. Eventually, the male coaxes her to the nest. Spawning usually occurs at a water temperature of 60° to 65°F, about 3 degrees cooler than the typical spawning temperature of largemouth bass.

As the spawning act begins, the fish lie side by side, both facing the same direction. Then the female tips on her side to deposit her eggs and the male simultaneously releases his milt. Females deposit an average of 7,000 eggs per pound of body weight.

The female leaves after spawning, but the male remains and vigorously guards the nest against any intruders. He will attack fish much larger than himself and may even bump a wading fisherman who gets too close. The amount of time required for hatching depends on water temperature. At 54°F, the eggs hatch in 10 days; at 77°, 2 days. On the average, 35 percent of the eggs hatch.

MALES *guard the fry (small black spots in the foreground) to protect them against predators, particularly small panfish. The fry are transparent when first hatched. They have a large, yellowish egg sac that nurtures them through the first 6 to 12 days of life. The black coloration begins to appear within a few days after the fry hatch. This explains the origin of the term "black bass."*

FINGERLINGS *are 3 to 5 inches long by the end of the first summer. The tail fin has a brownish orange base and a distinct whitish margin.*

"HOMING PIGEONS" OF THE FISH WORLD?

The homing tendency of smallmouth bass is among the strongest of all freshwater gamefish.

Each spring, small-mouth return to the same area to spawn. Even high water does not discourage them from returning to their traditional spawning sites. So once you find a spawning concentration, you can bet the smallmouth will be there again the next year.

In a lake or reservoir, a smallmouth may spend most of its time along a stretch of shoreline only 100 yards long. In a stream, a smallmouth may stay in one pool that fulfills all its needs for food and cover.

Smallmouth may leave these home areas to find good spawning habitat or a deep wintering area, but during the rest of the year they stray very little.

The wintering areas remain the same from year to year. In late fall, when the water temperature drops below 50°F, fishermen familiar with the water know exactly which sharp-dropping points and steep breaks will hold the smallmouth.

Weather

Weather plays a major role in smallmouth fishing. If you had a choice of when to fish, your odds would undoubtedly be best during a period of stable weather. Changes in the weather disrupt the smallmouth's feeding schedule. They may continue to feed, but peak feeding times are not as predictable. Exactly how changes in weather affect smallmouth depends on time of year, type of water, and even type of cover. Following are the weather conditions that have the most influence on smallmouth fishing:

CLOUD COVER. Smallmouth normally bite better when the skies are overcast rather than clear. Although smallmouth are not as light-sensitive as walleyes, low light causes them to move to shallow water and feed more heavily. But clear weather is nearly always better in early spring, because the sun warms the water and urges smallmouth to begin feeding.

The degree to which cloud cover affects smallmouth fishing depends on the clarity of the water. In lakes that are extremely clear, daytime fishing is usually poor when skies are sunny. In these waters, smallmouth do much of their feeding at night. But in lakes of moderate clarity, they feed sporadically throughout the day even though the skies are clear.

WIND. Windy weather generally spells good smallmouth fishing. The waves scatter the light rays so less light penetrates the surface and smallmouth feeding increases.

In a shallow body of water, a strong wind stirs up the bottom, making the water so murky that smallmouth cannot see well enough to feed. Fishing remains slow until the water starts to clear.

Windy weather may also cause poor fishing when smallmouth are in the weeds. The movement of the vegetation caused by the wave action seems to make them extra-cautious.

RAIN. Rainy weather usually improves smallmouth fishing, especially when the surface is calm. Overcast skies combined with rain droplets dimpling the surface decrease the amount of light that penetrates. And the sound seems to make the fish a little less spooky.

Rain has practically no effect on fishing on a windy day. Because light penetration is already low and the level of background sound is high, smallmouth are not as spooky as in calm weather.

A warm rain in early spring can make a big difference in fishing success. The water temperature may rise several degrees in one day, resulting in an insect hatch, which causes semidormant smallmouth to start feeding.

A heavy rain usually means poor fishing in streams. Runoff clouds the water so smallmouth cannot see your bait as well. And rising water spreads the fish over a larger area, so finding them is more difficult.

FISH INLETS IN THE RAIN

During and after a light rain, smallmouth often congregate around inlets, because the increasing flow attracts baitfish and washes in a variety of invertebrate foods.

In spring, the inflowing water may be several degrees warmer than the water in the lake or river, making the inlet even more attractive.

This situation makes for an excellent fly-fishing opportunity, because the fish are in shallow water, where you can easily reach them with a streamer and a floating line.

Storms accompanied by lightning and loud thunderclaps cause smallmouth to stop biting. Fishing stays slow for several days if the storm is severe.

COLD FRONTS. Smallmouth often go on a feeding spree before a storm, but if the temperature drops dramatically and the skies clear following the storm, catching them becomes tough.

The negative effects of a cold front are most noticeable in spring and summer, especially if the front follows a period of warm, stable weather. Smallmouth feed heavily during the warm weather, so they can afford to stop for a few days after the cold front passes.

Cold fronts usually do not slow feeding in fall. In fact, it seems as if smallmouth sense the approach of winter and begin fishing more heavily. Anglers willing to brave the elements can enjoy some of the year's best fishing.

COLD FRONTS *affect smallmouth in clear lakes to a greater degree than those in murkier lakes or rivers. This rule holds true for most other freshwater gamefish, as well.*

How Wind Affects Smallmouth Fishing

CROSSWINDS *blowing over the underwater extension of a point or over a reef wash plankton and insect larvae loose from the bottom and carry them to the downwind side. The drifting food attracts baitfish and smallmouth.*

ONSHORE WINDS *wash plankton in to shore and churn up the water, causing a mud line. Baitfish move in to feed on the plankton, and the light level is low enough for smallmouth to feed in the shallows.*

ROUGH WATER *scatters the light rays that strike the surface, causing much less light to penetrate than if the surface were calm. The lower light level causes smallmouth to move shallower and feed.*

Current moving through narrows

WIND-INDUCED CURRENTS *draw smallmouth into narrows and into troughs between islands or between an island and the lakeshore. The current attracts baitfish and the narrows or trough concentrates them.*

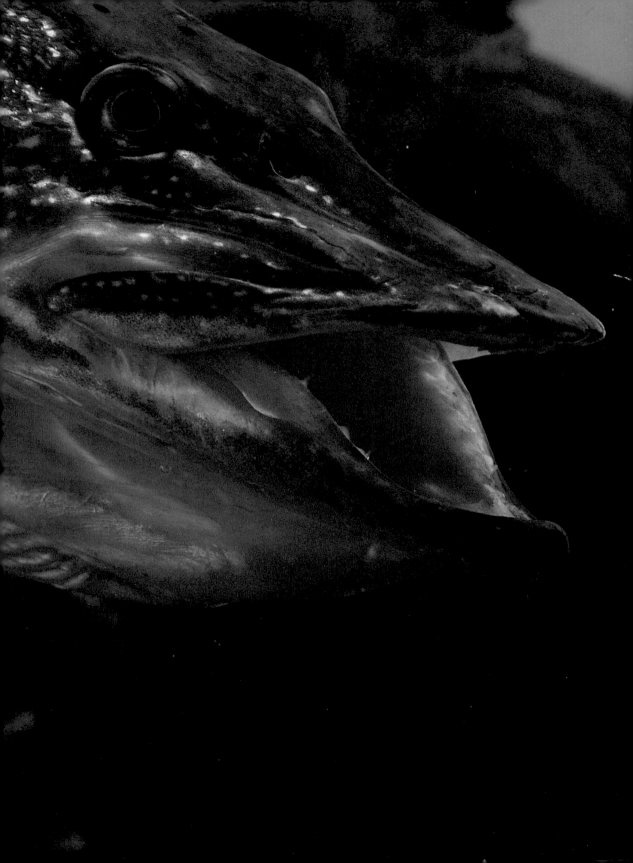

PIKE & MUSKIE

Pike & Muskie Basics

A sea of misinformation surrounds the northern pike and muskel-lunge. Even today, we hear stories of huge pike or muskies attacking swimmers or charging outboard motors. Such tales make good copy in magazine articles, but only serve to perpetuate the "evil" image of these fish.

Of course, pike and muskies are the top predators in any body of water, and they'll eat larger prey than most other freshwater fish. But they're not the ruthless killers they're commonly portrayed to be.

NORTHERN PIKE (Esox lucius) - Also known as northern, great northern pike, jack, jackfish, pickerel, brochet, luce, gator, snake.
The sides vary from
dark green

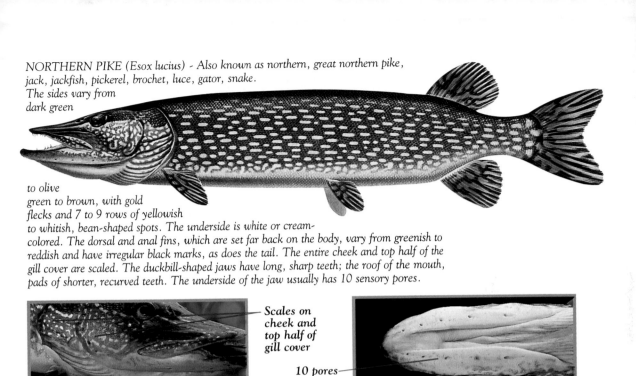

to olive
green to brown, with gold
flecks and 7 to 9 rows of yellowish
to whitish, bean-shaped spots. The underside is white or cream-
colored. The dorsal and anal fins, which are set far back on the body, vary from greenish to reddish and have irregular black marks, as does the tail. The entire cheek and top half of the gill cover are scaled. The duckbill-shaped jaws have long, sharp teeth; the roof of the mouth, pads of shorter, recurved teeth. The underside of the jaw usually has 10 sensory pores.

Scales on
cheek and
top half of
gill cover

10 pores

MUSKELLUNGE (Esox masquinongy) -
Also called muskie, lunge, maskinonge and innumerable other local
names.

Resembles the
pike in most respects, but the
background color of the sides is light,
rather than dark, and the tips of the tail are
more pointed. The sides vary from greenish
to brownish to silvery, usually with dark
markings, but the marks may be absent.
The white or cream-colored belly often has
brownish or grayish spots. The fins vary
from greenish to brownish to bloodred and
usually have dark markings. The cheek
and gill cover have scales only on the top
half. The number of pores on the underside
of the jaw varies from 12 to 20, but the
count is usually 15 to 18.

No scales

12 to 20
pores

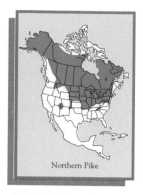

Northern Pike

Muskellunge

To become a proficient pike or muskie angler, one must put aside the backlog of misinformation about these fish and learn more about their behavior and biological requirements.

Northern pike and muskellunge, along with pickerel, are sometimes referred to as Esocids; they belong to the pike family, whose technical name is Esocidae.

Pickerel also belong to the pike family, but are much less popular with anglers because of their smaller size. Chain pickerel seldom exceed 5 pounds; redfin pickerel, 1 pound.

Northern pike hybridize with all other species of Esocids. The best-known of these hybrids, the tiger muskie, is a pike-muskie cross. Tiger muskies, which get their name from their distinct vertical bars (opposite), are rare in nature, because pike spawn so much earlier than muskie.

But fish hatcheries can easily produce hybrids, and the fish have been widely stocked in the United States. "Hybrid vigor" makes them grow faster than either parent, at least for the first several years of life. Tigers do not reach the ultimate size of purebred muskies because their life span is shorter.

MUTANTS AND HYBRIDS

SILVER PIKE. A mutant form of northern pike, the silver pike occurs throughout the pike's native range. The sides vary from bright silver to metallic blue or green and have no markings except silver or gold flecks on the scales.

Although pike and muskie have a great deal in common, their differences far outweigh their similarities. Pike occur naturally at northern latitudes throughout the world. Muskies, however, are native only to North America, and their range does not extend as far north.

Muskies seldom reach the population density of pike. Although they deposit just as many eggs, the hatch rate is lower, and because pike hatch earlier, they prey heavily on young muskies.

Technically, both species are classified as coolwater fish, meaning that they prefer lower temperatures than warmwater fish such as bass, but higher than coldwater fish such as trout. In reality, however, their temperature preferences differ considerably.

Muskies prefer water in the 67- to 72-degree range; small pike, a degree or two lower. But large pike (30+ inches) could almost be classed as coldwater fish, favoring water temperatures from 50 to 55 degrees. Pike also spawn and feed at lower temperatures than muskies. Another difference: pike bite throughout the year; muskies are seldom caught in winter.

Compared to pike, muskies are considerably more selective as to what they eat. They're known for their habit of following a fly, then

TIGER MUSKIE (pike-muskie hybrid). Sides with irregular, narrow bars, often broken into spots, on a light greenish to brownish background. The tips of the tail are rounder than a muskie's. Usually has 12 to 13 jaw pores.

turning away at the last second. But muskies can afford to be choosy; pike can't. Since muskies aren't as numerous, they face less food competition from other members of their breed. Pike must eat whatever they can whenever they can or be outcompeted.

Due to their finicky nature, muskies are commonly billed as "the fish of 10,000 casts." Stories often describe how an angler fishes for years to catch a single muskie. Such tales discourage many anglers from trying for muskies. It's true that muskie fishing can be tough, but it's not nearly as difficult as many writers would lead you to believe. Some muskie specialists land dozens each season.

Because pike aren't as selective, they're much easier to catch. In a creel survey conducted on a Wisconsin lake, anglers removed 50 percent of the pike crop in a single season. Another reason pike fishing is easier: the fish don't seem to learn from past mistakes. Many anglers have caught a pike with a distinctive marking, released it and then caught it again the same day. Rarely does this happen with muskies.

The relative ease of catching northern pike makes them extremely vulnerable to overfishing. In most heavily fished waters, pike exceeding 10 pounds are unusual. But in remote areas, they commonly reach 25 pounds or more. Muskies are less affected by fishing pressure and frequently attain weights in excess of 35 pounds, even in waters pounded by anglers.

The largest pike taken by fly fishing weighed 33 pounds, 8 ounces. It was caught in Nejanilini Lake, Manitoba, in 1994. Surprisingly, the largest fly rod muskie weighed only 18 pounds, 9 ounces. It was caught in Pike Lake, Wisconsin, in 1989. A tiger muskie caught in the St. Lawrence River, Quebec, in 1985, weighed 30 pounds, 6 ounces.

All Esocids are excellent food fish, with lean, white, flaky, mild-tasting meat. They're often belittled because of the Y-bones in the meat, but the bones can easily be removed. Muskies, however, are too scarce to kill for the meat. Release them to fight another day.

The Muskie Triangle

Muskie literature commonly refers to three distinct color phases – clear, spotted and barred. But anglers know that many of the fish don't quite fit any of these categories. The muskie triangle demonstrates how variable muskie coloration can be. At the points of the triangle are each of the distinct color phases; along the sides, intergrades between two color phases; in the center, a combination of all three.

BARRED. *The sides have dark, vertical bars that are wider than those of a tiger muskie and not as broken.*

CLEAR/BARRED. *The sides have dull bars that get progressively darker toward the tail.*

SPOTTED/CLEAR/BARRED.
The sides are almost clear at the front, but grade into a mixture of bars and spots that get darker toward the tail.

SPOTTED/BARRED. *The sides have a combination of spots and bars; spots are prominent toward the rear.*

CLEAR.
The sides and fins have no spots or blotches.

CLEAR/ SPOTTED.
The front of the body is mostly clear; spots are more prominent toward tail.

SPOTTED.
The sides and fins have roundish spots or blotches that are randomly spaced.

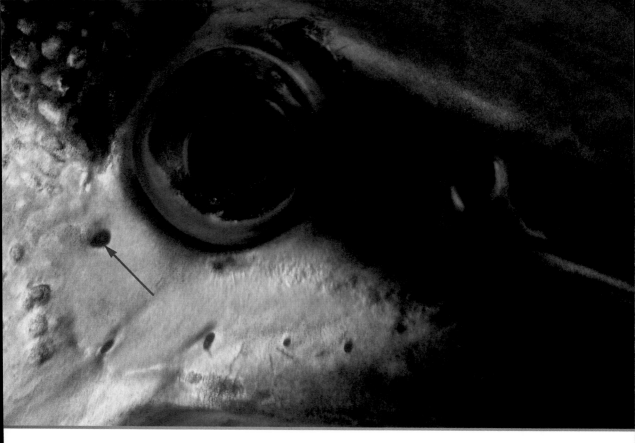

Senses

Like most top-level predators, Esocids depend strongly on sight to find food. Their eyes are highly movable, enabling them to track fast-swimming prey and to see in practically any direction. The photo sequence on pages 76-77 demonstrates how a pike follows its prey with its eyes.

Evidence suggests that muskies are even more sight-oriented than pike. Muskies do not fare well in low-clarity waters, while pike thrive in murky lakes and rivers. Dutch researchers captured the same blind pike in the wild on 3 successive years; evidently the fish was feeding normally. In the early 1900s, German researchers blinded pike by cutting their optic nerves. Afterward, the pike could still catch live baitfish, presumably using their other senses.

Muskies seem to have better night vision than pike, judging by the fact that they're relatively easy to catch at night. Pike, on the other hand, are seldom caught after dark. Night feeders generally have a high ratio of rods (light receptors) to cones (color receptors) in their retinas. There have been no studies to determine this ratio in muskies, but the ratio in pike is quite low, indicating a strong tendency toward daytime feeding.

Almost as important as vision is the lateral-line sense. An Esocid's lateral-line system includes lengthwise rows of pores along each side, as well as pores scattered on the underside of the jaw (p. 69). Slight vibrations in the water, such as those produced by swimming baitfish, activate tiny hairs inside the pores. The hairs, in turn, stimulate nerves inside and enable the fish to home in on its prey, even in murky water or under dim-light conditions. The lateral-line nerves in the head are especially important. The blinded pike mentioned earlier could not catch live baitfish after the nerves in their head were severed.

Reliance on their lateral-line sense explains why pike and muskies are drawn to big flies that produce a lot of vibration, such as the Dahlberg Mega-Diver. "Hardware" fishermen rely heavily on large-bladed spinnerbaits. Many anglers contend that you can often entice the fish to strike by changing the blades, and thus the pitch, of spinner-type lures.

The sense of smell is less important to pike and muskies than to most other freshwater fish. The lining of their nasal sacs has comparatively few lamellar folds and thus less surface area, so their sense of smell is less acute. One researcher studying the olfactory capability of pike concluded that they are totally devoid of the capacity to respond to the smell of food.

But this conclusion is probably an overstatement. During coldwater periods, live-bait fishermen frequently catch pike on dead baitfish, especially oily ones such as smelt, which have a strong odor. Muskies, on the other hand, rarely take dead baitfish.

1 A 6-inch pike in an aquarium rests motionless on the bottom when not feeding.

2 When a small minnow is dropped into the water, the pike immediately rotates its eyes in the minnow's direction and assumes an alert posture. Keeping its eyes on the minnow, the pike begins to swim upward.

3 Stalking the minnow, the pike moves slowly toward it while keeping its eyes riveted to the target.

4 Strikes occur at incredible speed. The pike takes the minnow and heads back to its resting position.

Spawning

Northern pike and muskies are random spawners, not nest builders. They scatter their eggs in shallow water, most often over live or decaying aquatic plants or their roots.

Before spring breakup, pike in many lakes swim up tiny streams to spawn in adjacent marshes, which are ice-free. When the water temperature reaches 40° to 45°F, they deposit their eggs in water only 6 inches to 3 feet deep. In lakes without spawning marshes, pike spawn in weedy bays shortly after ice-out. Muskies spawn 2 to 5 weeks later, normally at water temperatures from 49° to 59°F. Seldom do they move into the spawning marshes used by pike. They often spawn in the same weedy bays of the main lake, but in slightly deeper water.

Males move onto the spawning grounds a few days earlier than females. Spawning lasts for 5 to 10 days. As the eggs and milt are released, males thrash their tails wildly, evidently to help scatter the eggs. The violent activity commonly results in deep gashes and split fins and may even kill the fish.

Soon after depositing their eggs, females leave the spawning area. Males stay around for several weeks, but do not protect the eggs. With no parents guarding them, the eggs are vulnerable to predators such as crayfish and small fish. The eggs that survive hatch in about 2 weeks. After their mouths develop, the fry begin feeding on plankton.

Pike eggs hatch at a much higher rate than muskie eggs. Pike eggs sink slowly and are adhesive, so they cling to vegetation. Muskie eggs sink more rapidly and are not adhesive, so many of them settle into the mud and die from lack of oxygen.

In waters with both species, pike fry get a head start because of the difference in spawning time. Consequently, they're larger and can easily prey on muskie fry. When selecting waters to stock with muskies, fisheries managers look for lakes and rivers with relatively low pike populations. Otherwise, muskie fry wouldn't survive.

Anglers should understand how the spawning cycle affects fishing. Pike and muskies feed during the days before spawning and are catchable until spawning begins. They're seldom caught when spawning is in progress, but they start to bite again soon after it is completed.

PIKE FRY prey on the younger, smaller muskie fry.

The whereabouts of large female muskies, however, is a mystery in the weeks after spawning. Some anglers believe that they go deeper or suspend in open water, but nobody knows for sure.

Feeding & Growth

Writings like those of Botsford (left) have contributed to the widespread misunderstanding of muskies and pike. Often called "water wolves," these toothy predators inspire wild visions in the minds of the uninformed. As a result, many anglers have the attitude that the fish shouldn't be stocked in their waters for fear of wiping out bass, walleyes and other "more desirable" gamefish. The following discussion summarizes the latest research into the feeding habits and growth of pike and muskies.

FEEDING HABITS. In reality, pike and muskies consume about the same amount of food in comparison to their weight as most other freshwater fish. What probably kindles so many fantasies is the way these fish feed. The young do not hesitate to attack other fish of nearly their own size, grabbing the prey by the head and swimming about with the tail sticking out of their mouth until they digest enough to swallow a little more. Occasionally, one of them chokes on the oversized food and dies with the prey lodged in its throat. Adult pike and muskies will eat fish from one-fourth to one-half of their own length, and up to 20 percent of their own weight.

Shortly after hatching, pike and muskie fry start to feed on plankton. As they approach an inch in length, they begin feeding on tiny insects. At about 2 inches, they switch to a diet consisting mainly of small fish, including their own kind.

Throughout the rest of their life, fish continue to make up the bulk of their diet, but they will eat practically anything within the acceptable size range, including frogs, crayfish, mice, muskrats and ducklings. There have been reports of big pike and muskies attacking small dogs and even humans, although many such stories are greatly exaggerated.

How Pike and Muskies Take and Swallow Food

1 Large prey is digested gradually by Esocids. This sequence shows a small northern pike ingesting a shiner about one-third its own length. The pike grabs the prey crosswise, puncturing it with long, sharp teeth until it stops struggling.

2 It then turns the shiner and begins to swallow it head first. But the shiner is much too large to be swallowed completely right away.

3 The pike swallows as much of the shiner as it can, letting the tail protrude from its mouth while the front end is being digested.

4 As digestion continues, only the tip of the shiner's tail is visible. Sometimes the tail still protrudes from the mouth 24 hours after the prey was taken.

Given a choice, both northern pike and muskies would choose a soft-finned, cylindrical-bodied forage fish, such as a sucker, over a deep-bodied, spiny-rayed fish, such as a sunfish. The latter type would be harder to swallow and more likely to lodge in their throat. But in reality, pike and muskies eat plenty of sunfish, perch and other spiny-rayed fish, probably because they're commonly found in typical Esocid habitat.

Once Esocids grab their prey, patches of sharp, recurved teeth on the roof of their mouth (photos, right) and their tongue prevent it from escaping while they gore it with their larger teeth, which have extremely sharp edges.

Because pike and muskies feed mainly by sight, they're most active in daylight hours. But in clear lakes, or in waters with heavy fishing pressure or lots of boating activity, muskies do much of their feeding at night.

ESOCIDS are considered "sprint predators." They usually lie in wait in some type of cover, intently observing their prey. At the opportune moment, they cock their body into an "S," then dart forward, striking the prey at speeds approaching 30 miles per hour.

As experienced pike and muskie anglers know, the fish feed most heavily in overcast weather. Under sunny skies, they turn on just before sunset, although there may be a burst of feeding activity in early morning. Fishing is generally better with a light-to-moderate chop than a glassy surface. An approaching storm spurs a flurry of activity. Muskies turn off after a cold front, but pike continue to feed.

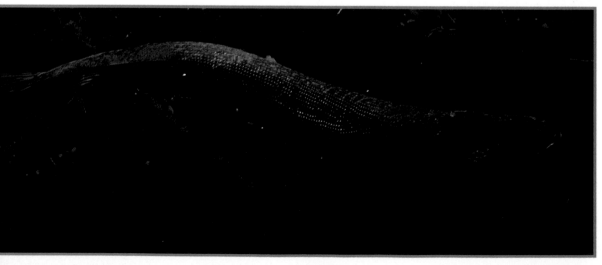

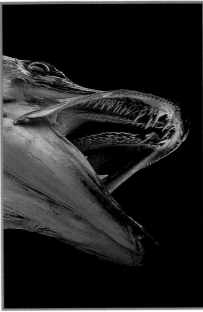

TEETH of Esocids are ideal for holding and killing prey. The dentary teeth, seen on the lower jaw of this mounted pike (left), pierce the prey while the tooth pads on the roof of the mouth prevent it from escaping. A muskie (right) has larger canine teeth on the roof of its mouth, which are ideal for holding bigger prey.

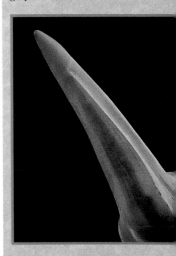

The peak feeding temperature for adult northern pike is about 65°F. The fish do some feeding throughout the year, but once the water temperature exceeds 75° in summer, the quantity of food they consume drops dramatically.

Poor summertime pike fishing is mainly a result of this feeding slowdown, not loss of teeth as many anglers believe. If pike can find cooler water, however, they will continue feeding.

Pike go on a feeding binge from late fall to early winter, presumably to nourish developing eggs and testes. By midwinter, however, the fish become much less active and food consumption drops to about 10 percent of the maximum level.

Although muskies are occasionally taken in the winter, they feed very little until the water warms to 50°F in spring. Feeding peaks at about 70°, and some feeding continues until the water reaches 80°. The fish consume more food as the water cools in fall, but they seldom feed once the water temperature drops below 40°.

GROWTH. How fast pike and muskies grow and the ultimate size they attain varies tremendously from one body of water to another. In many lakes, pike become so numerous that they dramatically reduce the crop of forage fish, resulting in severe stunting. Lakes with plenty of high-fat forage, such as ciscoes or smelt, produce considerably fewer pike, but the fish are big and deep bodied.

Although anglers often accuse muskies of cleaning out all the forage in a lake, rarely do the fish become numerous enough to cause a food shortage. As a result, stunting is a far less serious problem with muskies than with pike.

Water temperature also affects growth. Pike grow fastest at a water temperature of about 66°F; muskies, about 73°.

The rapid growth of northerns in cool water explains why deep lakes usually produce bigger pike than do shallow ones. In summer, shallow

Fast-Growing vs. Slow-Growing Pike

FAST-GROWING pike (top) have deep, wide bodies, often with relatively small heads. Slow-growing pike, commonly called "hammer handles" (bottom), have very skinny bodies and comparatively large heads.

lakes warm uniformly from top to bottom, so pike cannot find cool water. When forced to live at temperatures well above their comfort range, they grow slowly and their life span is much shorter than normal. In warm water, pike seldom live more than 6 years; muskies, 12. But in cool water, both species may live 25 years or more. The Canadian record muskie, a 65 pounder, was determined to be 30 years old.

Pike reach a maximum size about two-thirds that of muskies. The North American record pike weighed 46 pounds, 2 ounces; the record muskie, 69 pounds, 11 ounces. Pike from Europe and Asia approach the muskie's maximum size. The largest well-documented Eurasian pike weighed 67 pounds, 4 ounces.

On average, Eurasian pike outweigh North American pike of the same length by about 13 percent. Pike genetics differ very little throughout their range, so it's uncertain why Eurasian pike are heavier-bodied.

GROWTH RATES OF MUSKIE AND PIKE AT DIFFERENT LATITUDES

	Length in Inches at Various Ages (Years)										
Muskie	1	2	3	4	5	6	7	8	9	11	13
Maskinonge Lake, ON (50° N)	-	-	22.0	24.1	27.2	27.4	27.7	29.1	30.1	34.5	-
Lac Court Oreilles, WI (46° N)	8.6	15.3	20.5	24.8	27.2	29.8	31.6	33.0	36.4	-	-
Kawartha Lakes, ON (44° N)	6.9	17.5	23.7	28.1	31.2	34.3	36.6	38.6	40.4	43.5	46.0
Conneaut Lake, PA (42° N)	6.7	15.0	21.5	27.0	31.1	34.7	37.7	40.5	44.6	47.2	50.4
Piedmont Lake, OH (40° N)	15.5	22.3	29.9	33.7	36.3	38.2	40.9	43.0	47.3	-	-
Pomme de Terre Lake, MO (38° N)	12.2	22.1	29.1	35.2	36.7	39.7	42.2	45.5	-	-	-
Northern Pike											
Great Slave Lake, NWT (62° N)	4.2	6.3	8.6	11.1	13.2	15.5	17.5	19.6	21.3	24.7	28.6
Saskatchewan River Delta, SK (54° N)	4.2	8.9	14.7	19.7	22.0	23.1	24.8	27.3	31.5	-	-
Savanne Lake, ON (48° N)	9.6	13.8	16.6	19.3	21.7	24.4	27.3	30.8	33.5	36.5	-
Lake Vermilion, MN (47° N)	7.6	12.8	16.8	19.9	22.5	25.6	29.0	32.7	34.6	38.9	-
Lake Mendota, WI (43° N)	11.4	21.3	26.9	30.3	33.7	36.3	37.9	39.1	-	-	-

Habitat

The circumpolar distribution of northern pike reflects their ability to adapt to many kinds of habitat. Their North American range extends from 40° to 70°N, well above the Arctic circle. They've been widely stocked throughout the Great Plains and Rocky Mountain states.

Pike exist in practically every type of water, from warm, shallow ponds, to deep, cold lakes, to muddy rivers. They even live in brackish areas of the Baltic Sea. Their broad tolerance for water temperature, water clarity and dissolved oxygen content makes them one of the most adaptable freshwater fish species.

Although pike, especially good-sized ones, prefer cool water, they can endure temperatures into the low 80s. But if they cannot find cool water in summer, they grow slowly and don't live long. Pike can tolerate very low clarity and oxygen levels and are among the last gamefish to die when a lake winterkills.

Muskies also inhabit a variety of lakes and rivers, but they're not nearly as versatile as pike. Found only in North America, their native range extends from 36° to 51°N, barely reaching into Canada.

Like pike, muskies can survive in a wide range of water temperatures. But they're seldom found in waters with a maximum water temperature below 68°F. They can tolerate water temperatures up to the mid 80s. Muskies prefer clear water and cannot adapt to water that stays turbid most of the time. They require considerably higher oxygen levels than pike.

Both species prefer shallow, weedy water (less than 20 feet deep) during their early years of life. But as they grow larger, they spend more time in deep water. This tendency is stronger in pike than in muskies.

Pike and muskies will not put up with fast current, so they're seldom found in rivers with a gradient of more than 10 feet per mile. But if there are backwater areas where they can get out of the moving water, they'll live in rivers with higher gradients and faster currents.

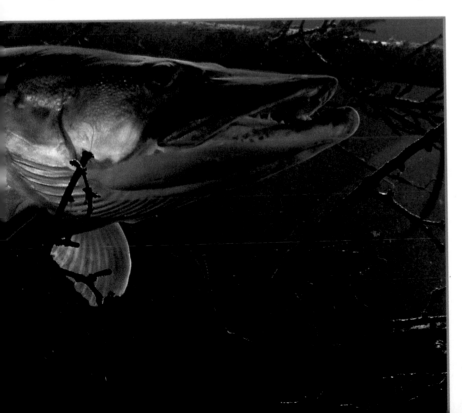

Weather

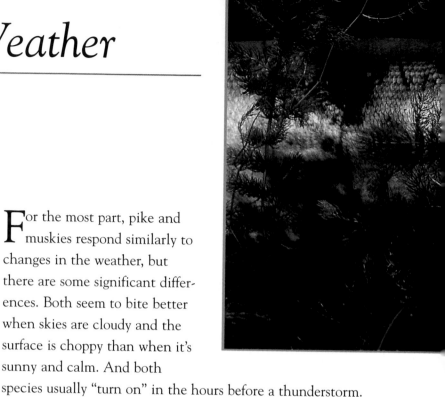

NOT THE TIME FOR EXPLORATION

When a cold front slows fishing, the tendency is to start looking for the fish in new locations.

But chances are the fish are right where you've been catching them; they just aren't feeding.

It's best to stick with your proven spots, returning to them every couple of hours.

Try placing your fly as close to the cover as possible, sometimes bumping it to "wake up" the fish.

For the most part, pike and muskies respond similarly to changes in the weather, but there are some significant differences. Both seem to bite better when skies are cloudy and the surface is choppy than when it's sunny and calm. And both species usually "turn on" in the hours before a thunderstorm.

Rainy weather usually improves fishing, but a heavy rain can slow the action on a river. If too much mud washes in and clouds the water, these sight feeders have difficulty spotting your fly.

In windy weather, muskies often feed heavily along the windward shore, where baitfish move in to feed on the windblown plankton. But pike fishing may actually be better along the lee shore, where upwelling cool water from the depths draws feeding pike (right).

It takes a severe cold front to slow the pike action, but even a mild cold front can shut down the muskies. The colder temperature, often coupled with a strong northwest wind, pushes the fish off the structure or causes them to bury themselves in weedy or woody cover. Feeding activity subsides as insect hatches stop and baitfish move out of the shallows.

The effects of a cold front are most noticeable on clear lakes, especially in spring when the fish are in shallow water. River fish are not immune to cold fronts, but show less response than lake fish.

COLD FRONTS *drive muskies, and sometimes pike, into dense weeds.*

The best way to cope with cold front conditions is to do your fishing from late afternoon until just after dark, the time when the water temperature normally peaks. This may be the only time of day when the fish feed. It also pays to fish a little deeper than normal, because the ultraclear skies following a cold front allow the sun's rays to penetrate deeper.

WAIT for an offshore wind to catch summertime pike in stratified lakes. An offshore wind pushes warm water away from shore, and cooler water from the depths wells up to replace it. The water temperature along the lee shore may drop several degrees, enough to draw pike into weedbeds and other cover along shore where the water had previously been too warm.

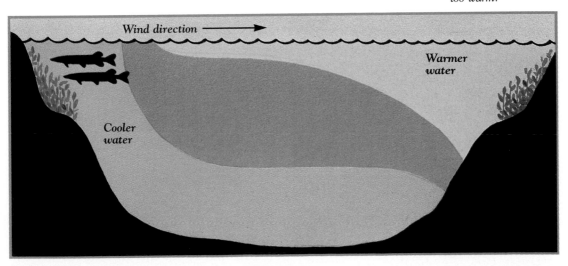

Wind direction ⟶

Warmer water

Cooler water

SUNFISH

Sunfish Basics

The name sunfish refers to the bright, sunny colors of these scrappy fighters. This chapter will include only true sunfish, members of the genus *Lepomis*, but the sunfish family also includes crappies, large-mouth and smallmouth bass, rock bass and other fishes not called sunfish.

The bluegill, redear, pumpkinseed, redbreast and longear are the most popular sunfish. Many other types of true sunfish do not grow large enough to interest anglers.

Sunfish can adapt to most any type of water, with the exception of cold lakes and streams. They live in small ponds, natural lakes, reservoirs and river backwaters. Most sunfish species seek out warm, shallow, slack-water areas. Some kinds, like the redbreast, prefer flowing water.

Sunfish have a strong homing instinct and return to spawn in the same vicinity each year. Males choose a nest site, then use their tails to sweep the bottom clear of debris. A typical spawning bed measures 1 to 2 feet in diameter and several inches deep. The beds appear as round, light-colored spots on bottom. Sometimes the nests are so close together they form one massive spawning colony. After deposit-ing their eggs, females abandon the nests. The males remain for sev-eral days to guard the eggs and newly hatched fry from predators.

Some species of sunfish produce so many young that they overpopu-late a lake or pond. An individual spawning bed may contain as many as 200,000 fry. If a high percentage of young fish survive, they deplete their food supply, resulting in a population of stunted fish. Overpopulated lakes seldom produce keeper sunfish. The largest fish usually come from lakes with relatively low numbers of sunfish.

Sunfish eat larval and adult insects, invertebrates, mollusks and small fish. They rely heavily on their senses of scent and sight to find food. Although they usually feed in morning and early evening, they may also feed during midday. Sunfish bite in sunny or cloudy weather.

WHAT KIND OF FISH IS IT?

Sunfish commonly crossbreed, resulting in hybrids that have some characteristics of both parents. Hybrids may cross with other hybrids or with their parents. Even experienced biologists have trouble identifying fish from a hybridized population. Small hybrid sunfish are a nuisance in many lakes. But some hybrids are superior to the parent fish. For example, redear sunfish, when crossed with green sunfish, produce a fast-growing, hard-fighting hybrid.

Bluegill

DOUBLE YOUR FUN

For shallow-water bluegills, try a popper, along with a nymph dropper. Tie an 8-inch piece of tippet material slightly lighter than your main tippet to the bend of the popper hook, then tie on the nymph. Aggressive bluegills will take the popper; others may hit the nymph. Often you'll catch fish on both flies.

Bluegills are the most widespread and abundant sunfish species. They were originally found only in the eastern half of the United States, but stocking has expanded their range to include every state except Alaska. They are sometimes called sun perch, bream, sunfish, copperbelly or roach.

The gill cover has a powder-blue fringe, and the "ear flap" is entirely black. The sides have about 5 dark, vertical bars that may be vague, and the rear base of the dorsal fin has a dark blotch. The pectoral fin is long and sharply pointed.

Bluegills are considered superb eating. The meat is white, flaky, firm and sweet.

94

HABITAT. The best bluegill populations occur in clear waters with moderate weed growth, such as shallow lakes and slow-moving portions of streams. If there are too many weeds, bluegills tend to become stunted, because the cover affords protection from predators for too many of the young. Large bluegills are usually found in deeper water than small ones. Bluegills prefer water temperatures from 75° to 80°F.

FOOD HABITS. The diet consists mainly of larval and adult insects, plankton, snails and fish fry. They sometimes eat bits of aquatic plants. Bluegills feed on the surface, in the middle depths or on the bottom.

SPAWNING HABITS. Bluegills spawn in spring, usually at water temperatures from 68° to 70°F. They may spawn several times each year, with some spawning continuing into the summer. Spawning activity is heaviest from a few days before the full moon to a few days after. The male builds a nest on a sand or gravel bottom, often near other bluegill nests. After spawning, he guards the eggs and fry.

AGE & GROWTH. Bluegills live up to 11 years in the North, but seldom longer than 6 in the South. The growth rate varies greatly, depending mainly on population density. They may never exceed 6 inches in lakes where they are stunted, but may reach 10 inches (about 1 pound) in 4 years in lakes with a moderate population and a good food supply. The fly rod world-record bluegill weighed 2 lbs., 12 oz. and was taken in Guilford County, North Carolina, in 1984.

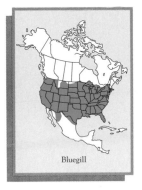

Bluegill

BLUEGILL VARIETIES

Northern Bluegill
(Lepomis
    macrochirus
        macrochirus)

Florida Bluegill
(Lepomis
    macrochirus
        mystacalis)

NORTHERN BLUEGILLS have brownish to greenish sides. The female has a yellowish breast; the male, orangish.

FLORIDA BLUEGILLS are dark bluish to greenish on the back with lighter sides. The male (shown) has a copper-colored patch above the eye that becomes more distinct at spawning time. This explains why the fish are sometimes called "copperheads."

Redear Sunfish

Known as the *shellcracker* to most southern anglers, the redear sunfish grinds up snails with a special set of teeth in its throat. Redears are also called stumpknockers, bream and yellow bream.

The sides of a redear are light olive-green to gold, with red or orange flecks. The black ear flap has a bright red or orange margin, explaining the species' name. Redears resemble pumpkinseeds, but are less colorful and lack the bluish streaks on the cheek. Males and females are similar in appearance, although the color on spawning males becomes more intense and the breast turns bright yellow or yellow-orange. The meat is similar in taste to that of the bluegill.

Redear Sunfish
(Lepomis microlophus)

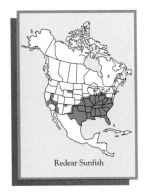

Redear Sunfish

HABITAT. Redears prefer clear, quiet water with moderate vegetation. Rarely are they found in moving water. They tolerate brackish water better than other sunfish but are intolerant of cold water, explaining why they are not found in the North. They prefer a water temperature in the 73° to 77°F range.

FOOD HABITS. Important food items include snails, larval insects and fish eggs. Redears are less surface oriented than most other sunfish, doing the majority of their feeding on the bottom.

SPAWNING HABITS. Redears spawn in late spring or early summer, generally at water temperatures from 66° to 70°F. Males build nests on sand-gravel bottoms or on softer bottoms along the edge of lily pads or submerged weeds. The male guards the eggs, then guards the fry after they hatch.

AGE & GROWTH. Redears grow faster than any other true sunfish and reach the largest maximum size. In some waters, limit catches of 1- to 2-pounders are commonplace. In most waters, redears grow to 1 pound in approximately 6 years. Their maximum age is about 8 years. The fly rod world-record redear weighed 2 pounds, 7 ounces and was caught in Merritt's Mill Pond, Florida, in 1989.

Longear Sunfish

LONGEAR VARIETIES

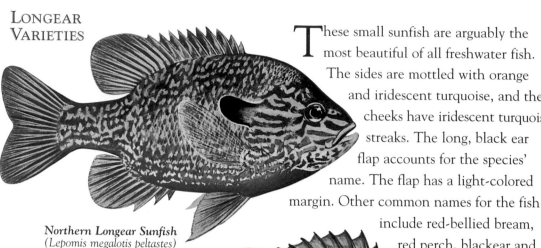

Northern Longear Sunfish
(*Lepomis megalotis peltastes*)

NORTHERN LONGEARS *have a long ear lobe that angles upward. The lobe often has a single red or orange spot. Northern longears, the smaller of the two, are found in the southern Great Lakes area.*

CENTRAL LONGEARS, *the predominant variety, have a very long ear lobe that is nearly horizontal. The margin of the lobe may have several reddish spots. On spawning males (shown) the turquoise coloration becomes almost fluorescent and the belly becomes an intense rusty orange. Central longears are found throughout most of the longear range.*

Central Longear Sunfish
(*Lepomis megalotis megalotis*)

Longear Sunfish

These small sunfish are arguably the most beautiful of all freshwater fish. The sides are mottled with orange and iridescent turquoise, and the cheeks have iridescent turquoise streaks. The long, black ear flap accounts for the species' name. The flap has a light-colored margin. Other common names for the fish include red-bellied bream, red perch, blackear and bream. Longears have white, flaky meat and are considered excellent eating.

HABITAT. Longears are most common in clear, shallow, slow-moving streams with moderate vegetation and a sand, gravel or rubble bottom. They are also found in warmwater lakes, reservoirs and ponds. They prefer water temperatures of 75° to 80°F, but can survive at temperatures up to 100°.

FOOD HABITS. Longears feed mainly on immature aquatic insects, worms, crayfish and fish eggs. They sometimes take adult insects on the surface.

SPAWNING HABITS. Spawning takes place in summer, normally at water temperatures from 70° to 74°F, but longears sometimes spawn at temperatures as high as 85°. Males build nests over a gravel bottom, often in colonies. After spawning, they guard the nest until the fry disperse.

AGE & GROWTH. The maximum life span is 9 years, but few longears live beyond 6. Most adults are only 4 to 6 inches in length. The central variety is the largest, occasionally reaching 9 inches. The world-record longear weighed 1 pound, 12 ounces and was caught in Elephant Butte Lake, New Mexico, in 1985. There is no fly rod record.

Redbreast Sunfish

Native to the Atlantic Coast states and as far north as New Brunswick, redbreasts have been stocked in many southern states. The redbreast is also called the yellowbelly sunfish, robin, redbelly and bream. Although the redbreast is one of the smaller sunfish species, it has white, flaky, sweet-tasting meat, much like that of the bluegill.

HABITAT. Redbreasts are found mainly in streams along coastal plains and can tolerate slightly brackish water. They prefer deep, slow-

Redbreast Sunfish

REDBREAST SUNFISH (Lepomis auritus). The golden brown sides have blue streaks and pale red spots. The black ear flap is as long as that of a longear sunfish, but it does not have a light-colored margin. The redbreast is named for the male's orange-red breast. Males also have olive-colored upper sides and blue streaks on the cheek. Females are less colorful, with pale red to yellowish breasts.

moving areas of clear streams, with boulders, logs, weedbeds or undercut banks for cover. They will not hold in fast current. They also live in lakes, reservoirs and ponds, particularly those with moderate weed growth. Redbreasts favor warm water, from 80° to 84°F.

FOOD HABITS. Common foods include aquatic and terrestrial insects, snails, crayfish and small fish. Redbreasts are more prone to night feeding than other sunfish. Primarily bottom feeders, they will also take food on the surface.

SPAWNING HABITS. Redbreasts spawn in late spring or early summer, usually at water temperatures from 66° to 70°F, but sometimes at temperatures as high as 82°. Males build nests on sand-gravel bottoms, generally near stumps, logs or rocks. They guard the nest until shortly after the fry hatch.

AGE & GROWTH. Compared to most other sunfish, redbreasts are slow-growing. They grow fastest in the South, but even there, they reach only about ⅓ pound in 6 years. They seldom live beyond age 7. The world-record redbreast weighed 2 pounds, 1 ounce and was caught in the Suwannee River, Florida, in 1988. There is no fly rod record.

Pumpkinseed

What the pumpkinseed lacks in size it makes up for in aggressiveness. These willing biters are among the most colorful of all sunfish. Also called common sunfish, yellow sunfish or bream, pumpkinseeds are excellent eating, much like bluegills.

PUMPKINSEED
(Lepomis gibbosus).
The golden sides have green, orange and red flecks, and iridescent blue and emerald reflections. The underside is bronze to red-orange. Wavy blue streaks mark the side of the head. The ear flap has a half-moon spot of bright red at the tip. Females have the same markings as males, but their colors are not quite as intense.

Pumpkinseed

HABITAT. Originally a fish of the north-central and eastern United States, pumpkinseeds have been stocked in many parts of the West. They prefer slightly cooler water than other sunfish, from 70° to 75°F. Pumpkinseeds thrive in small, shallow lakes, sheltered bays of larger lakes, or quiet areas of slow-moving streams. They're seldom found in expanses of open water. Pumpkinseeds inhabit shallower water and denser vegetation than bluegills and redears. They are not found in brackish water.

FOOD HABITS. Insects make up the bulk of the pumpkinseed's diet, but it eats many other foods, including snails and small baitfish. Pumpkinseeds have smaller mouths than most other sunfish, which explains their habit of nibbling at baits. They will take food on the surface or on the bottom.

SPAWNING HABITS. Spawning takes place in late spring or early summer, usually at water temperatures from 66° to 70°F. Males build

the nests on a sand or fine-gravel bottom, usually at depths of 6 to 18 inches, and guard the eggs and fry.

AGE & GROWTH. Pumpkinseeds are unusual in that they grow slightly faster in the northern part of their range than in the southern part, probably because of their preference for cool water. On average, it takes about 8 years for a pumpkinseed to reach ½ pound. The maximum life span is about 10 years. The world-record pumpkinseed weighed 1 pound, 6 ounces and was caught in Oswego Pond, New York, in 1985. There is no fly rod record.

OTHER FLY ROD SPECIES

Crappies

Crappies rank near the top with panfish anglers because they are easy to catch and live in a wide variety of waters.

There are two species of crappies: black and white. Depending on the region, fishermen refer to both types as specks, papermouths, bachelor perch, white perch, calico bass and many other colorful names.

PRIME CRAPPIE TIME

Look for early-spring crappies in shallow, dark-bottomed bays, boat harbors, back-channels or any other water that warms quickly. The fish will be in water only a few feet deep and can easily be taken on wet flies, nymphs or small streamers.

Another prime time for fly fishing is later in the spring, when the fish start to spawn. When the water temperature reaches the low 60s, crappies move into bulrushes or other emergent vegetation that grows on a hard bottom. If the water is clear enough, you may be able to sight-fish for them.

Fly fishing gets much tougher after spawning, because crappies scatter into deeper water.

Crappies belong to the sunfish family. They have flat, silvery bodies with black to dark green markings. These markings vary in intensity, depending on the time of year and type of water. During the spring spawning period, a male black crappie may appear jet black over much of its body. Markings on male white crappies darken around the head, breast and back. Crappies from clear waters usually have bolder patterns than fish from murky waters.

The original range of black crappies included most of the eastern half of the United States, with the exception of New England. They have been introduced in many western states and even British Columbia. White crappies were originally found within a region extending from

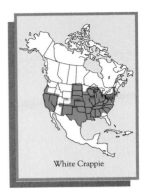

White Crappie

Black Crappie

eastern South Dakota to New York, then south to Alabama and Texas. They have been introduced as far west as California.

HABITAT. Although black and white crappies share many of the same waters, black crappies are most abundant in cool, northern lakes with gravel or sand bottoms. They are almost always found around vegetation.

Both species live in rivers and streams, but black crappies prefer quieter waters. They can tolerate a higher salt content, which explains why they are more common than white crappies in estuaries along the East and Gulf coasts.

BLACK CRAPPIE (Pomoxis nigromaculatus). The sides are silvery with a greenish to yellowish cast and scattered dark specks. The dorsal fin has 7 or 8 spines. Black crappies are deeper-bodied than whites and have a less noticeable depression in the forehead.

White crappies are most common in reservoirs, lakes, rivers and bayous of the South.

WHITE CRAPPIE (Pomoxis annularis). The sides are silvery with emerald and purple reflections and 7 to 9 dark vertical bars. The dorsal fin usually has 5 or 6 spines. White crappies are more elongated than blacks and have a deeper depression in the forehead.

They can tolerate murkier water than black crappies and can thrive in basins with either soft or hard bottoms. They usually live near some type of cover.

FOOD HABITS. Both black and white crappies have a large number of *gill rakers*, bony projections in the gills that are used to strain plankton from the water. Crappies also eat small fish, insects, mollusks and crustaceans. In many southern reservoirs, they feed heavily on gizzard and threadfin shad.

More sensitive to light than sunfish, crappies feed most heavily at dawn, dusk or at night. They bite throughout the year, but feed less often once the water drops below 50°F.

SPAWNING HABITS. Crappies spawn earlier than any other member of the sunfish family. They usually nest when the water temperature reaches 62° to 65°F, which can be as early as January in the Deep South or as late as June in the North.

Spawning crappies prefer gravel bottoms, but will nest on sand or mud if gravel is not available. They also spawn on boulders, dense mats of plant roots and shell beds. Most nest in weeds or brush, or near logs and other large objects. In streams, they often spawn beneath overhanging banks.

Males are the first to arrive on the spawning grounds and the last to leave. They establish and defend a territory, then build a nest by fanning away debris. After the female deposits her eggs, the male stays to protect the nest. The eggs hatch in 3 to 5 days, depending on the water temperature.

Most crappies spawn in water 2 to 10 feet deep. But nesting fish have been seen in water from several inches to 20 feet deep. As a rule, the larger the fish, the deeper it spawns. In waters where both species are found, white crappies normally spawn slightly deeper than blacks. Spotting crappie nests can be difficult, because their beds are not as distinct as those of sunfish.

AGE & GROWTH. Crappie populations fluctuate dramatically in most waters, resulting in highly variable growth rates. On the average, it takes approximately 7 years for the fish to reach a weight of 1 pound in the North; 5 years in the South. Black crappies have a longer maximum life span than whites – 10 years vs. 8 years – but, in reality, few crappies survive past age 5. The fly rod world-record black crappie weighed 2 pounds, 13 ounces and was caught in Custis Millpond, Virginia, in 1994. The fly rod world-record white crappie weighed 2 pounds, 8 ounces. It was taken in Amelia County, Virginia, in 1986.

CRAPPIE CYCLES

For reasons that nobody really understands, crappie populations are highly cyclical. Once every 3 to 5 years, an unusually large percentage of young crappies survive. They grow slowly because so many fish compete for a limited food supply. As a result, anglers catch only small fish for 2 or 3 years. But once predation, angling pressure and natural mortality reduce the population, the growth rate increases and fishermen enjoy a year or two of good fishing for large crappies.

Rock Bass

Many anglers know the rock bass as the goggle-eye or redeye, names derived from the fish's bulging, reddish-colored eyes. The rock bass is a member of the sunfish family, but is not a true bass.

The original range of the rock bass covered the eastern half of the United States and into southern Canada, with the exception of states

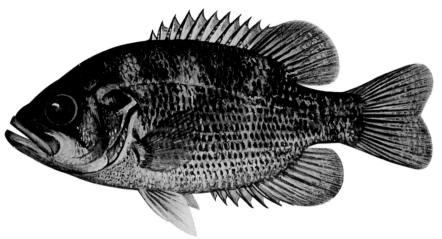

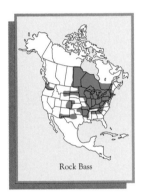

Rock Bass

along the eastern seaboard. Rock bass have been stocked in states both east and west of their native range.

The meat has a good flavor, but is commonly infested with parasites, especially in clear northern lakes.

HABITAT. Rock bass prefer clear weedy lakes and ponds, and clear, slow-moving streams. They are usually found over a rocky bottom; seldom over a silty one. They prefer water temperatures from 69° to 74°F.

FOOD HABITS. Aquatic insects, crayfish and small fish make up the bulk of the diet. Rock bass do most of their feeding near the bottom, but sometimes take adult insects off the surface.

SPAWNING HABITS. Rock bass spawn in late spring or early summer, at water temperatures in the upper 60s. The male builds the nest in very shallow water, usually over a coarse sand or gravel bottom. After spawning, he guards the eggs and fry.

AGE & GROWTH. Rock bass grow slowly, but live up to 13 years. In the North, it takes about 9 years for the fish to reach ½ pound; in the South, 7 years. The all-tackle record rock bass, caught in the York River, Ontario, in 1974, weighed 3 pounds. There is no fly rod record.

FINNY CHAMELEONS

Rock bass have the unique ability to camouflage themselves by changing color, much like a chameleon. Their dark brown mottling may disappear in seconds, leaving only the plain tan or greenish background color.

White Bass

Few gamefish provide as much angling excitement as white bass. The silvery fish cruise about in schools that may cover several acres. The schools, or *packs*, often push baitfish to the surface or into confined areas, and the fish then slash into their prey. If you can find

one of these rampaging schools, you'll probably catch a fish on every cast. Circling gulls may tip you off to a pack's location.

White bass are easily spooked by a boat, so when you find a school, keep your distance or the fish will quickly disappear.

Originally found in the Great Lakes, the St. Lawrence River and the Mississippi River System, white bass have been successfully stocked in many other parts of the country, particularly the Southeast and Southwest. Commonly introduced in new reservoirs, they provide excellent fishing starting 2 or 3 years after stocking.

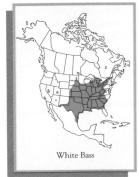

White Bass

Lake Whitefish

Anglers have just started to recognize the lake white-fish as a worthy fly-rod opponent. The fish are good-sized, readily take flies and are considered excellent eating, both fresh and smoked, although the meat is a bit on the oily side.

Lake whitefish are members of the trout/salmon family, and like their relatives, are coldwater fish. A dwarf form of the species occurs in some northern lakes. Lake whitefish are also called common whitefish.

HABITAT. Lake whitefish are found in the cold depths of oligotrophic lakes, often sharing habitat with lake trout. In the Great Lakes, they have been taken in nets at depths as great as 420 feet. In the Far North, they can survive in shallow

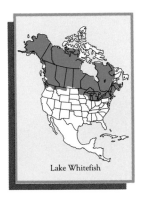

Lake Whitefish

lakes, because the water stays cool year-round. Whitefish prefer water temperatures of 50° to 55°F.

FOOD HABITS. Primarily bottom feeders, lake whitefish eat insect larvae, mollusks, fish eggs and small fish. But during a hatch, they can often be seen taking insects on the surface.

SPAWNING HABITS. Lake whitefish spawn in late fall or early winter, usually in shoal areas of large lakes, but occasionally in tributary streams. Spawning begins at a water temperature of about 43°F. The fish do not build nests, but broadcast their eggs over a gravelly or stony bottom. The eggs incubate over winter and hatch the following spring.

AGE & GROWTH. The growth rate of lake whitefish varies greatly from one body of water to the next. In the southern part of their range, they generally reach a weight of 2 pounds in about 4 years; in the northern part, it may take 11 years to reach that size. But the growth rate may differ greatly even in adjacent lakes, possibly due to genetic differences. Whitefish have been known to live as long as 28 years, although anything over 15 is unusual. The fly rod world-record lake whitefish weighed 4 lbs., 15 oz. It was taken in the Winnipeg River, Manitoba, in 1986.

LAKE WHITEFISH (Coregonus clupeaformis). The silvery sides have large scales and no markings. The body is more flattened than that of its close relative, the mountain whitefish, and the snout is more underslung.

FAST& FURIOUS ACTION

On calm summer mornings and evening, you'll often see acres of whitefish dimpling the surface as they feed on midges and other tiny insects that are hatching. Tie on a dry fly about the size and color of a hatching insect and you'll often get a hit on every cast.

American Shad

American Shad

L ike striped bass, American shad spend most of their lives at sea, but spawn in freshwater streams. During the spring spawning run, they move into coastal rivers, often in spectacular numbers. Although they do not feed after entering fresh water, they eagerly take flies and other artificial lures.

Also called white shad, Atlantic shad and common shad, American shad are feisty fighters, commonly cartwheeling from the water several times before tiring. They are

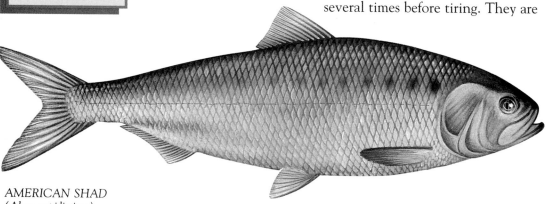

AMERICAN SHAD (Alosa sapidissima). The sides are silvery, with large, loose scales and a row of black spots behind the gill cover that become smaller and less distinct toward the tail. The upper and lower jaws are nearly equal in length. The closely related hickory shad has a lower jaw that projects well beyond the upper.

considered good eating, and the roe is eaten fresh and used for caviar.

American shad are native to the Atlantic coast. But in the late 1800s, they were stocked in several rivers along the Pacific coast. They are now found in coastal rivers from central California to Southeastern Alaska.

HABITAT. Found in fresh water only during the spring spawning run, American shad swim up rivers along the Atlantic and Pacific coasts. They cannot tolerate cold water and avoid water temperatures below 41°F.

FOOD HABITS. The diet of the American shad consists mainly of plankton, which is filtered from the water by the gill rakers. Other foods include crustaceans, small fish and fish eggs.

SPAWNING HABITS. American shad spawn as early as mid-November in Florida, and as late as July in Canada. Most spawning activity takes place at night, commencing at a water temperature of about 54°F and peaking at about 65°. The eggs are released near the surface and allowed to drift with the current. In the northern part of their range, American shad return to the sea after spawning; in the southern part, they die.

AGE & GROWTH. Although American shad occasionally live up to 11 years, very few survive past age 7. First-time spawners, which are about 5 years old, generally weigh 3 to 5 pounds. Repeat spawners range from 5 to 9 pounds. Females generally grow faster than males. The fly rod world-record American shad weighed 7 lbs., 4 oz. It was caught in the Feather River, California, in 1983.

SHAD SECRETS

•*Look for schools of shad in deep channels and long, slow pools.*

•*Fish during low-light conditions – in early morning, evening or in overcast weather.*

•*Use small flies in clear water; large ones in dark water.*

•*Don't apply too much pressure when fighting shad. The hook tears out easily because of their soft mouths.*

123

Night Fishing,
  Brown trout, 21
  Redbreast sunfish, 101
Northern Bluegill, 95
Northern Largemouth, 33
Northern Pike,
  About, 68, 69, 70-72
  Digestion process, 81
  Distinguishing from muskie, 69,
    71, 72
  Feeding and growth, 71-72, 80-85
  Feeding temperature, 83
  Fishing in spring, 71
  Fishing pressure, 72
  Food competition, 72
  Growth rate, latitudes (chart), 85
  Habitat, 86-87
  Hatch rate, 79
  Identifying, 69
  Lateral line, 74, 75
  Myths about, 68, 80
  Range, 70
  Roaming behavior, 87
  Senses, 53, 74-77
  Spawning, 71, 78-79
  Teeth, 83
  Use of sight, 76-77
  Water temperature preferences,
    71, 82
  Weather, 88-89
  World record, 72

O

Oncorhynchus, 10
Oncorhynchus aguabonita (Golden
  Trout), 14
Oncorhynchus clarki bouvieri
  (Yellowstone Cutthroat Trout), 13
Oncorhynchus clarki clarki (Coastal
  Cutthroat Trout), 13
Oncorhynchus clarki henshawi
  (Lahontan Cutthroat Trout), 13
Oncorhynchus clarki lewisi (West Slope
  Cutthroat Trout), 13
Oncorhynchus gorbuscha (Pink
  Salmon), 17
Oncorhynchus keta (Chum
  Salmon), 17
Oncorhynchus kisutch (Coho
  Salmon), 16
Oncorhynchus mykiss gairdneri (Brown
  Trout), 12
Oncorhynchus mykiss irideus
  (Steelhead), 12
Oncorhynchus nerka (Sockeye
  Salmon), 17
Oncorhynchus tshawytscha (Chinook
  Salmon), 16
Oxygen Requirements, 56
  Bass, 41, 56

Panfish, 56
Pike, 56
Salmonids, 27, 56

P

Pacific Salmon, 10
  Identifying, 11
  Spawning, 22
Packs, 112
pH, 56
Pickerel, 69, 70
Pike, see: Muskie, Northern Pike
Pink Salmon,
  Range, 17
  Spawning, 25
  World record, 17
Pomoxis annularis (White
  Crappie), 108
Pomoxis nigromaculatus (Black
  Crappie), 108
Pores,
  Northern pike and muskie, 69,
    74, 75
Pumpkinseed,
  About, 102
  Age and growth, 103
  Feeding, 102
  Habitat, 102
  Range, 102
  Spawning, 102-103
  Water temperature
    preferences, 102
  World record, 103
Put-and-Take Stocking, 10

R

Rain,
  And bass behavior, 45, 63
  Effect on fishing, 47
Rainbow Trout, 25
  Habitat preferences, 26
  Identifying, 10
  Spawning, 22, 25
  See also specific subspecies
Red-Band Rainbow Trout,
  Range, 12
  World record, 12
Red Salmon, see: Sockeye Salmon
Redbreast Sunfish,
  About, 100
  Age and growth, 101
  Feeding, 101
  Habitat, 100-101
  Night feeding, 101
  Range, 101

Spawning, 101
Water temperature
  preferences, 101
World record, 101
Redear Sunfish,
  About, 96-97
  Age and growth, 97
  Distinguishing from
    pumpkinseed, 97
  Feeding, 97
  Habitat, 97
  Range, 97
  Spawning, 97
  Water temperature preferences, 97
  World record, 97
Rock Bass,
  Age and growth, 111
  About, 110, 111
  Feeding, 111
  Habitat, 111
  Range, 111
  Water temperature
    preferences, 111
  Spawning, 111
  World record, 111

S

Salmo, 10
Salmo salar (Atlantic Salmon), 16
Salmo trutta (Brown Trout), 12
Salmon,
  About, 8-10
  Identifying, 11
  Range maps, 16-17
  Senses, 18, 19
  Spawning, 10, 22
  Species, 16, 17
  Water temperature preferences, 9
  See also specific species
Salmonidae, 10
Salmonids, 10
  Catch-and-release, 10
  Identification, 11
  Put-and-take stocking, 10
  Range maps, 12-17
  Species, 12-15
  Spawning, 25
  Water temperature preferences, 9
  See also: Salmon; Trout;
    specific species
Salvelinus, 10
Salvelinus alpinus (Arctic Char), 15
Salvelinus confluentis (Bull Trout), 15
Salvelinus fontinalis (Brook Trout), 14
Salvelinus malma (Dolly Varden), 15
Salvelinus namaycush (Lake Trout), 15
Sand Bass, 114
Shad, see: American Shad

Shellcracker, see: Redear Sunfish
Silver Bass, 114
Silver Pike, 70
Smallmouth Bass,
    About, 50-51
    And competition, 57
    And low water level, 59
    Color phases, 51
    Crayfish in diet, 58
    Distinguishing from largemouth, 51
    Feeding and growth, 58-59
    Fishing in spawning beds, 60
    Growth rates at various latitudes
        (chart), 59
    Habitat, 54-57
    Homing tendency, 61
    Identifying, 50, 51
    Lateral line, 52
    Range, 50
    Senses, 52-53
    Spawning, 60-61
    Water temperature preferences, 54,
        55, 60
    Weather, 62-65
    World record, 51
Smell (Sense of),
    Bass, 35, 53
    Panfish, 53
    Pike, 53, 75
    Salmonids, 19, 53
Smolts, 24
Sockeye Salmon,
    Range, 17
    Spawning, 25
    World record, 17
Spawning,
    Bass, 38, 39, 60, 61, 111, 115, 117
    Crappies, 109
    Pike, 78, 79
    Salmonids, 10, 22-25
    Shad, 123
    Sunfish, 95, 97, 99, 101
    Walleye, 119
    Whitefish, 121
Steelhead,
    Range, 12
    World record, 12
Stizostedion vitreum (Walleye),
    118, 119
Stocking, 10, 113
Striped Bass,
    About, 116
    Age and growth, 117
    Feeding, 117
    Habitat, 116-117
    Hybrid, 116
    Pack feeding, 117
    Range, 116
    Spawning, 117
    Water temperature
        preferences, 117

World record, 117
Striper, 114
Structure,
    And bass, 42, 43
Sunfish,
    About, 93
    Bluegill, 94-95
    Crappies, 106-109
    Homing instinct, 93
    Hybrids, 93
    Identifying, 94-102
    Longear sunfish, 98-99
    Pumpkinseed, 102-103
    Redbreast sunfish, 100-101
    Redear sunfish, 96-97
    Water temperature preferences, 93

T

Tadpoles, 58
Temperature Preferences, see: Water
    Temperature Preferences
Thymallus articus (Arctic
    Grayling), 14
Tiger Muskie, 70, 71
    World record, 72
Trout,
    About, 8-10
    Anadromous, 10, 29
    Best trout water, 27
    Feeding and growth, 21
    Habitat, 26-27
    Identifying, 11
    Lateral line, 19
    Predators, 8, 24
    Range maps, 12-15
    Senses, 18-19, 53
    Spawning, 22
    Species, 12-14
    Tippet visibility, 19
    True, 10
    Water temperature preferences, 9,
        26, 29
    Weather, 28-29
    World record, 12-15
    See also specific species

V

Vision,
    Of bass, 35, 53
    Of panfish, 53
    Of pike, 53, 74-77
    Of salmonids, 18, 19, 53

W

Walleye,
    About, 118-119
    Age and growth, 119
    Feeding, 119
    Habitat, 119
    Range, 118
    Spawning, 119
    Water temperature
        preferences, 119
    World record, 119
Walton, Sir Izaak, 68
Warm Fronts, 44
Water Clarity, 27, 57
Water Fertility, 41
Water Temperature Preferences, 9
    Of bass, 37, 38, 41, 54-56
    Of panfish, 56
    Of pike, 56, 71, 83, 87
    Of salmonids, 26, 56
    Of various fish (chart), 56
Weather,
    And bass, 44, 45, 62-65
    And pike, 88, 89
    And salmonids, 28, 29
    See also specific weather patterns
West Slope Cutthroat Trout,
    Range, 13
    Spawning, 25
White Bass,
    About, 112-114
    Age and growth, 115
    Dams, fishing below, 115
    Feeding, 114
    Habitat, 114
    Hybrid, 114
    Range, 113
    Spawning, 115
    Water temperature
        preferences, 114
    World record, 115
White Crappie, 107, 108
    See also: Crappies
Whitefish, 10
    See also: Lake Whitefish
Wind,
    And bass behavior, 45, 63, 65
    Effect on fishing, 47
Winterkill, 41
Wipers, 114, 116
World Record,
    American shad, 123
    Arctic char, 15
    Arctic grayling, 14
    Atlantic salmon, 16
    Bluegill, 95
    Brook trout, 14
    Brown trout, 12
    Bull trout, 15
    Chinook salmon, 16

Chum salmon, 17
Coho salmon, 16
Crappie, 109
Dolly Varden, 15
Golden trout, 14
Lahontan cutthroat trout, 13
Lake trout, 15
Lake whitefish, 121
Largemouth bass, 33
Longear sunfish, 99
Northern pike, 72
Pink salmon, 17
Red-band rainbow trout, 12
Redbreast sunfish, 101
Redear sunfish, 97
Rock bass, 111
Salmon, 16, 17
Sockeye salmon, 17

Smallmouth bass, 51
Steelhead, 12
Striped bass, 117
Sunfish, 103
Tiger muskie, 72
Trout, 12-15
Walleye, 119
White bass, 115
Wiper, 117

Y

Yellowstone Cutthroat Trout,
  Range, 13
  Spawning, 25

Photo Credits

*Note: **T**=Top, **C**=Center, **B**=Bottom, **L**=Left, **R**=Right, **I**=Inset*

©**Photo Researchers, Inc.**
/Ted Clutter,
p.24T.

©**Roger E. Peterson,**
p.61T.

©**Andy Anderson,**
p.62.

©**Steve Probasco,**
p.68, p.117.

© **In-Fisherman,**
p.73TC, p.73BC.

©**Joe Bucher,**
p.73BL.

©**Doug Stamm,**
p.100.

©**Dan D. Gapen, Sr.,**
p.120.

©**Richard Franklin,**
p.123.